SLAY DOUBT!

How to recognise and confidently manifest God's calling on your life.

DETOLA AMURE

SLAY DOUBT!

How to recognise and confidently manifest God's calling on your life.

Super Working Mum
Copyright © 2019 'Detola Amure
First published in 2019 by Aloted Inc Limited

Edited by: Oluwaseun Ibiyemi
Book Cover design and layout by: Graceful Living Ltd.

ISBN-13: 978-1-7897240-42

Printed in the United Kingdom

WHAT READERS ARE SAYING ABOUT SLAY DOUBT!

Slay Doubt is a timely blend of biblical and everyday wisdom tips for today's woman. I believe it is a complete guide for every woman who seeks to maximize purpose in the midst of the many things she has to juggle and contend with. The practicality of the book on our relationship with God and how we can draw strength from Him to scale life's hurdles and succeed in every area of our lives is exceptional.

Detola has generously shared her experiences, successes and setbacks in driving home the points. Her style of writing makes it easy to comprehend and implement the lessons. I appreciate how she has intricately blended her personal experiences with her knowledge of the scriptures to produce such an inspiring piece.

Every woman should read *Slay Doubt* and get running with the lessons already.

~Sola Adesakin, Wife and Mum of 3
CPA FCA FCCA MBA, Personal and
Business Finance Expert, Founder
and Lead Coach: The Smart Stewards

Each one of us has been called to greatness. Each one of us has a deposit of heaven that we need to spread on earth. Only the courageous dare to step out and fulfil this assignment while on earth. In the book, *Slay Doubt*, Detola opens our minds to see beyond our doubts, our current circumstances, our fears and inadequacies. Anchored in faith and hope, this book will shake your world if you've been making excuses and allowing your experiences in life shape your calling. Embrace God. Embrace your place. Embrace His strength and go do exploits!

~Mofoluwaso Ilevbare,
Wife and Mum of 2
Confidence Coach,
Founder, Flourishing Forties Network.

Many women deal with doubt by shutting the door to their minds. We allow our future actions to be shaped by the past and the present. This amazing life-giving book, *Slay Doubt,* explores the different phases of life we might be in and shows us biblically and practically how to recognise the doubt and fear holding us down and how to rise above it into our calling. A masterpiece!

Funmi Onamusi
Wife and Mum of 2
Founder, 3F EV Limited

Slay Doubt is a beautifully written book that applies to every season of a woman's life. Detola has accurately captured the struggles most women have to deal with as they grapple with pertinent life questions such as who am I? Is this all there is to life? Am I living only for others? Am I good enough?

This book takes you on an exciting journey on how to discover who you are in Christ, identify your own USP (unique selling point), develop a strategy for success, navigate different seasons without losing your vision and the importance of building a strong network of trusted friends. I hope more young women get to read this book as they begin their journey in life.

~Adenyke Israel-Bolarinwa
Wife and Mum of 3
Executive Director, Esther's Preparation Room

OTHER BOOKS BY DETOLA

Super Working Mum
Boosting Your Confidence
Journaling for Personal Growth

This book is dedicated to my children:
Moyo, Mojola, Morakinyo and Moradeyo.
I am privileged to be your mother.
With each pregnancy and birth I found my purpose.
Each one of you, in your own way, is teaching me what
life and purpose is really all about. I love you my darlings.

ACKNOWLEDGEMENTS

Abba Father, you are the potter, I am the clay. I am nothing without you. You have carried me through the good and bad times. Through it all, you have been faithful. Thank you choosing me even before the foundations of the earth. I hope I make you proud.

Jesus my big brother and friend, I love you. Holy Spirit, my counselor, comforter and advocate, thank you for *dynamis* power and strength to write this book even when I thought I couldn't do it.

TJ, my husband and friend, thank you for being my rock. Thank you for allowing me to follow my God-given dreams.

My parents: Deacon Dr. John Oyediran & Deaconess Mrs. Bolanle Olabisi, thank you for nurturing me in the way of the Lord. Thank you for your constant prayers. I feel them every day. I love you.

Toks Aruoture, thank you for your constant prayers, guidance and words of encouragement. I am blessed to have you in my life.

Coach Aaron T Aaron, working with you has transformed me and prepared me for the journey I have been on. Thank you for always bringing a fresh perspective to my thinking.

Oluwaseun Ibiyemi, thank you for editing this book and for improving this book from my raw thoughts to what people can actually read and digest.

Aji Michael, thank you for your creativity and thought process in putting this book together.

The *Super Working Mum Academy*, you are my found family and the nation God assigned to me. Thank you for allowing me to be a part of the journey of birthing your God-given dreams. I don't take this opportunity for granted. Thank you for being my spiritual and emotional support during traumatic seasons of my life.

A big thank you to the *Super Working Mum* community at large, all over the world. Because of you, the vision God gave me has found expression. I am grateful for your prayers and allowing me to serve you.

Toyin, Emilola, Ifueko and Diane thank you for agreeing to share part of your story in this book. Your stories really brought to life the message of manifesting God-given dreams. You all inspire me.

A big shout out to all my friends and prayer partners who have been a part of my journey. If I begin to mention names, I know I might miss out a few. I am truly grateful for every single one of you. God bless you.

CONTENT

FOREWORD

The subject of faith is one that cannot be separated from Christianity. Indeed, the start of our journey with Christ requires us to believe in a God we cannot see. Consequently, many books have been written on the subject, in an attempt to help us understand this concept. When Detola asked me to write the foreword of *Slay Doubt*, I was both honoured and excited. Words can be powerful but experience trumps words every time. Detola has shared from her heart what she has encountered in her journey both personally and as a life coach.

As sensual beings, we take our instructions mostly from what our senses perceive, or what our minds instruct us. This is our default state and puts a spanner in the works when it comes to living by faith - which calls us to ignore the senses and the emotions, and instead, live from the spirit. Our humanity craves engagement in the only way it knows how to, which is by communicating in the flesh.

One of the challenges we face is that our senses are daily being bathed by the antithesis of faith. It is difficult to believe when we are surrounded by evidence of the absence of what we hope for. Add to that the presence of a myriad of solutions and promises from well-meaning authors and preachers, which do not give practical reasons why our faith sometimes just does not work.

Detola addresses the subject of aligning the spirit, soul and body in the correct order. *"You are a spirit; you have a soul that lives in your body. The correct order flows from your spirit to your soul and then to your body. They should always be in alignment"*

Living by your spirit - which is one with God, lifts you to a plane that's higher than that of those living merely from the body or even the soul. This higher living allows you to create life, as opposed to reacting to the life you now have based on other people's decisions. We understand that you can either do as you please based on what your soul or body wants, or do as God pleases based on what your spirit wants.

Slay Doubt guides you in a step by step manner explaining the basics of faith through daily living along with the common obstacles we face. You will learn how to navigate life with the Holy Spirit as your partner. Often, we have an expectation of what our lives should look like as Christians, we therefore become frustrated when it looks nothing like what we have envisaged.

Through this beautifully written book, you will embrace your unique walk with God at a pace that He has chosen for you. The result is that you will create and live the life that God has intended for you, which is good and perfect. In addition, you will embrace the challenges because now you know that they are designed to shape you as you live by the leading of the Holy Spirit.

I have known Detola for many years and seen the consistency in her life's journey along with her extensive work with the *Super Working Mum Academy* and Super Working Mums all over the world. This qualifies her to teach on the subject of faith and confidence from a practical point of view. Her authenticity and desire to see women blossom in their own journey with God can be experienced between the pages of this book.

Slay Doubt is an easy read for anyone looking to move beyond having the title of being a Christian to the experience of a faith-filled life. It is a practical book as examples are drawn from real-life, everyday women and most chapters finish with action steps you can take. The message in this book is also backed up by the Word of God.

FOREWORD

I commend Detola on such a concise, yet comprehensible book.

Toks Aruoture
Wife and Mum, Businesswoman,
Inspirational Writer and Speaker.
www.toksaruoture.com,
www.thebabycotshop.com

READING THIS BOOK

I read a lot of books.

Some of the books I find very frustrating are those where more than half of the book rehashes what the problem is and then only a few chapters are dedicated to discussing the solution. When I read such books, I feel weighed down with the problems described and I can hardly find the energy or mental space to digest the solutions provided.

This book in your hands isn't one of those books.

I know you are likely to be a busy woman or mum and your time is very precious. I respect that, so I don't want to waste your time.

I know you already know what the problem is, if not, you won't be reading this book. The problem may present itself to you like this:

- You doubt that you have been called in the first place.

- You suspect God has called you, but you are full of doubt and fear.

- You are distracted by the affairs of life, so find it hard to recognise and own God's calling on your life.

- You are afraid and insecure because you don't think you have what it takes, or you are running away from your calling like Jonah did.

- You have belittled God's calling on your life, thinking 'the call' is only for Pastors or ministers of God.

■ You have experienced trauma or painful situations, and all you want to do is hide under a rock, lick your wounds and never come out.

The first part of this book touches on recognising and fully embracing the call of God on your life so that you can confidently manifest His call. Until you own the call, you will do nothing about the call, or quit when opposition or hardship comes your way.

In the second part of this book, we shall delve deeply into three seasons of life that could potentially hinder you from confidently walking in purpose. I share strategies on how to confidently manifest all that God has deposited within you during these seasons.

Living for God is the only way to live as a child of God. Any other way of living is a waste of the time, talents and gifts God has given you to use for His glory and to redeem others to Him.

In this book, I share my story and the relatable stories of some of the ladies I have coached or mentored, to help you uncover Holy Spirit inspired solutions that you can begin to apply today. Four ladies in the *Super Working Mum Academy* also share their personal stories of how they are continually slaying doubt and confidently manifesting God's calling on their different journeys.

You might find me repeating a number of truths in this book; this is because these truths need to sink deep into your subconscious. And when you know the truth, it shall set you free.

I have also included reflection questions and action steps in some of the chapters. I encourage you to get a journal to write down your thoughts and action steps as you read.

SCOPE OF THIS BOOK

This book assumes that you already have an idea of what God has called or mandated you to do, what I might also refer to as your *unique assignment* on earth.

You may already be on the path to fulfilling your unique assignment, but may have reached an obstacle and are not sure how to navigate the season you are in. You may just be starting out and are feeling overwhelmed about what to do. If you fall into either category, this book is for you.

If you are not sure of what your calling or unique assignment is, I will encourage you to check out the *Map Your Life Purpose Blueprint program* which will take you on a journey of identifying and embracing your life purpose.

It is an online course, which is part of the *Super Working Mum Academy* - an online community of women who are maximizing their time and manifesting their God given dreams. I share more details about this at the end of the book.

INTRODUCTION

L ooking back, I can say that God's hand has always been on my life, guiding me on my life's journey. I was born into a Christian home and first gave my life to Jesus when I was eight years old. I later rededicated my life to Jesus in secondary school when I was 13. However, I can say I only truly began to think about living a life of purpose and the fact that God had a call over my life at the age of 33. This is not to say that the 25 years following my initial encounter with Christ were a waste, or that I wasn't living for Jesus. I would say those years were part of my preparation time before I finally heeded the call of God. I went off tangent several times, but God's grace and mercy kept drawing me back.

When I gave my life to Christ, I responded to the first call i.e. I received God's gift of salvation through Jesus Christ and all the blessings that come with it. I belonged to Jesus Christ and partook in God's redemptive work on earth. Every person who has given his or her life over to Jesus has also responded to the first call.

When I say I started thinking of purpose and the call of God, what I mean is that I began to really recognise and understand that God had a unique assignment for me on earth, just like He does for you. When I was eight, my uncle noticed my writing skills and encouraged me to write more, which I did. At age 21, my youth pastor at my parent's church prophesied into my life telling me I was called to lead women. He declared that he could see me on a platform speaking to lots of women. When he told me this, all I could do was stare at him and wonder what he was going on about. I had just completed my first degree and wanted to get on with my life. You know, get a well-paying job, get married, have a bunch of children, etc.

I was a regular girl who did regular things; went to primary school, secondary school, and university. I even got a master's degree because that was the *'thing'* to do when you were born into a family that strongly values education; not that there is anything wrong with getting a master's degree.

During my master's program in Operational Research at Lancaster University, I began to think I had made a mistake pursuing the degree, but I followed through with it because *"I wasn't born to quit."* It was during this time that my first blog was born: *Purpose Driven Blog.* I think this blog and my love for writing kept me going during that one year of undertaking a rather tedious and strenuous master's program.

I had a good job with Accenture in Lagos, before going to study for my master's in the United Kingdom (UK), so I went back to work in Nigeria and continued progressing on the career ladder. I resigned some months later, came back to the UK and got a new job. I got married to my amazing husband and one year later got pregnant. And this was when my *'problem'* or should I say awakening happened.

Getting pregnant and having a baby at age 29 did something to me physically, emotionally and spiritually. I started getting restless and questioned this regular life I was living. There were only a few people I could share this with, as I didn't want anyone thinking I was crazy. I kept having this nagging feeling that there was more to life, but I didn't know what to do about it, so I kept on living my regular life.

I experienced some form of depression and lack of confidence in myself during my maternity leave. When I got pregnant, I stopped blogging and many other things I used to enjoy doing. I think pregnancy does that to you sometimes; it messes up your hormones, which can affect your daily life if you let it. I didn't want to go back to work - I dreaded going back, but I had to return to work because that was the *'regular thing'* to do and the bills had to be paid. Back at work, I kept having this nagging thought in my head: *"there has to be more to life than this."* Little did I know that God was trying to catch my attention.

Thankfully, I got my confidence back, which I share about in my book: *Boosting Confidence, 15 steps to success in the workplace.* I continued on this career path and was very good at it, but I knew deep down within me that there was more to life than work and paying bills. Anytime I brought this up with my husband, he didn't understand where I was coming from, so I carried on because this was what was expected of me.

Here I was, a new mum, with insecurities, struggling to juggle everything: marriage, taking care of a new baby, work, relationships, my spiritual and personal growth. I began to wonder what my life was really about. I was constantly feeling like I wasn't getting the balance right, and after talking to other mums, I realised it wasn't just me. A good friend of mine encouraged me to start a blog on being a career/working mum and finding the balance with everything else. I took on the challenge since it involved what I loved doing - researching and writing.

This new project got me really excited, I went straight to work, and this was how *Super Working Mum* was born. I am sure Abba was smiling down from heaven when I went to work, not knowing this was HIS idea and part of His unique call on my life.

I must say God's hand was on the blog from day one, seeing that it was His idea in the first place, delivered to me through a friend. I remember wondering what name I would call my new blog. I brainstormed all kinds of names and none was clicking. Then one day I was driving to work and I heard it: *"Super Working Mum"*. At first, I thought, *"hmm sounds like Super Mum"* which tends to have a negative connotation, where every woman is trying to be a superhero, but the name stuck, and I bought the domain name instantly.

The real meaning of the name *Super Working Mum* (*relying on the* **supernatural** *strength of the Holy Spirit to do all you need to do as a woman*) was revealed to me two years later as I walked deeper in my calling. This goes to show that Abba doesn't always show us the full picture of what He has called us to do from day one. As we respond to His call to our unique assignment, as we become more confident in stepping out of our comfort zone, He will begin to reveal more and more to us along the way.

On this journey of stepping into God's calling on my life, I have experienced depression, anxiety, lack of confidence and various kinds of attacks from the enemy along the way. I have felt discouraged and incapable; I have felt unqualified and disqualified so many times. I have experienced bouts of doubt on so many occasions, wondering if I was on the right path. I have thought about giving up and just going back to living an average life like many other people around me, but I am grateful that the grace of God has kept me on His chosen path for me.

You may have a similar or not so similar experience to mine when it comes to realising that you have a call of God on your life.

You may have been called to:

- *be a leader in the marketplace,*

- *set up a business that will provide solutions to people's problems,*

- *run a ministry to help orphans, widows, young boys & girls, the sexually abused or the bereaved,*

- *write life-changing books, create content, make movies,*

- *a political assignment to effect change in governmental policies,*

- *raise godly children; maybe even raise the next 'Martin Luther King Jr',*

- *rise in your career to make strategic decisions to transform organisations that will affect the common man.*

Others may have discounted you.
You may have felt unqualified or afraid.
You may have been ridiculed, opposed or persecuted.
You may have experienced doubt.

But

I am here to tell you that if I could do it, then so can you by the special grace of God. I hope that as I share what I have learned and am still learning on my journey with you, you will find some Holy Spirit inspiration, strategies, and tools to help you slay doubt and confidently manifest God's call on your life. I pray that you would allow Jesus to be Lord in every aspect of your life so that you will experience the fullness of what He has for you as you obey His call on your life.

I don't have all the answers, but what I do have is what Abba has been teaching me along the way, and this is what this book aims to share.

Let's have a conversation, sister to sister.

This book may simply be a reminder of what God is already telling you. Or this book may bring a fresh revelation, or a new perspective on what you already know. Whatever the case, open your heart because it is time to slay doubt and confidently manifest God's calling on your life.

A few things you might notice in this book

I call God "Abba" a lot. That's because I have come to recognise Him as my loving father, holding my hand every step of the way, teaching me and grooming me in the path He has laid out for me.

I refer to the Holy Spirit as Holy Spirit without *"the"*. Again, I am cultivating a personal relationship with Him. I won't call my dad *"the dad"* or my husband *"the husband"* or Jesus *"the Jesus"*. Do you catch my drift? ;)

Happy reading!

Blessings,
'Detola Amure.

SECTION 1

CHAPTER 1

WHAT IS GOD'S CALLING?

*B*efore you can confidently manifest God's calling on your life, you need to recognise what it is. Some people see their calling as their vocation or job, but your calling is much more than that. As a believer in Christ, you have been called out of darkness into God's marvelous light.

A calling according to the Bible means an invitation. God's call is the purpose for which you exist. It is the reason why you were created. It is God's mandate for your life…His assignment for you to do on earth.

Like I shared in my story, God's calling on your life starts when you make Jesus the Lord of your life.

Remember when Adam & Eve sinned in the Garden of Eden, we lost fellowship with God. God's plan was to redeem us back to Him from the Kingdom of Darkness into the Kingdom of Light, so that the fellowship that existed with Him before the fall can be restored.

So, the first calling from God is to every person on earth to receive His gift of salvation through Jesus Christ and all the blessings that come with it. This call is an invitation to surrender to Jesus Christ and partake in the redemptive work God is doing on earth. It is a call to be born again.

Unfortunately, not everyone will respond to this calling. When we respond to this call, we are translated from darkness into God's marvelous light. We are restored back to God and now have the commission to tell others about God's love through our gifts and talents, through a chosen and unique way God shows to us. I will share more on this later.

Your second calling - after you become born again - is to have an intimate relationship with God the Father, Son and Holy Spirit. It is to experience eternal life here on earth. Most people think eternal life begins only when we die and go to Heaven.

John 17:3 (NLT) tells us what eternal life is:

"And this is the way to have eternal life - to know you, the only true God, and Jesus Christ, the one you sent to earth."

Eternal life starts as soon as we give our lives to Christ. Eternal life begins with experiencing who God is on this earth.

Your third calling is that as you experience eternal life and the love of God, you tell others of the love of Jesus, through your unique assignment, so they can also believe and accept Him. This could also be termed as your earthly calling.

A lot of people, as they grow up, tend to focus on their earthly calling as a form of vocation or work to do. Whilst this is important, knowing and understanding the first two callings on our lives will help us fine-tune what our earthly calling should be.

As a child of God, you have a specific earthly calling on your life that ties back to God's redemptive plan. Through the help of God and the love of Jesus, you have been called to set a group of people free from whatever is blocking them from receiving eternal life. I call this group **'*your nation*'**.

So, you may ask, *"what does this look like on a day to day basis? How do I live out God's calling on my life?"*

Psalms 139:16 (NLT) says:

"You saw me before I was born. Every day of my life was recorded in your book. Every moment was laid out before a single day had passed."

This means everything pertaining to your life already exists in the spirit realm, and you now have a unique path to navigate what that looks like in the physical/earthly realm. This might translate to just ONE BIG assignment or several assignments that you discover on your life's journey with God.

For some, they discover from a young age what their unique assignment is through prophecies over them, through their natural gifts or through other means. While for some, it takes them going through some situations or a life-defining moment, for their unique assignment to be revealed. Whatever your case may be, as you take one step in trust and obedience, Abba will reveal more to you.

Many are called, few are chosen.

According to the Strong's Greek Concordance, the word 'chosen' means: *'elected', 'selected', 'picked out', 'chosen out by God' for the rendering of special service.*

This word 'chosen' is typically used for believers in Christ, in other words, Christians; people who have responded to the first calling as described earlier and have obtained salvation through Christ. So if you are a believer, it means you have been selected or elected by God to render a special service.

A couple of questions that may have crossed your mind are these:

"What is the special service I have been chosen to render?"
"How do I embrace that service with confidence and without doubting?"

The answers to the first question are addressed extensively in the *Super Working Mum Academy* program - *Map Your Life Purpose* that I mentioned earlier. The second question will be addressed in this book.

To buttress the point about God's calling on our lives, all believers in Christ have been chosen to declare God's praises on earth. We are all called to ministry.

Our first ministry is to God where we worship Him, give Him praise and develop an intimate relationship with Him.

Each believer has been given a special assignment by God to help others on earth, and when we fulfill this assignment, we ultimately bring praises and glory back to God.

How do I know for sure that you have a special assignment?

Because the Bible attests to this.

Isaiah 49:1 (NASB) says:

"Listen to Me, O islands,
And pay attention, you peoples from afar.
*The Lord **called Me** from the womb;*
From the body of my mother He named me."

Ephesians 1:4-6 (NASB):

*"Just as He **chose** us in Him before the foundation of the world, that we would be holy and blameless before Him. In love, He **predestined** us to adoption as sons through Jesus Christ to Himself, according to the kind intention of His will, to the praise of the glory of His grace, which He freely bestowed on us in the Beloved."*

Ephesians 2:10 (NASB):

*"For we are His workmanship, created in Christ Jesus for good works, which God **prepared beforehand** so that we would walk in them."*

Don't get bogged down

A lot of people get bogged down with the details of *"is my life's calling just one thing? If so, how do I know I haven't missed that one thing?"* This may cause fear and doubt, which stops them from making any move in life.

Like I mentioned before, when you give your life over to Jesus you are already walking in your calling and purpose. Isn't that amazing to know?

Then as you begin to develop an intimate relationship with the Trinity, your days recorded in God's book begin to unfold. You are now living for God and not for yourself. It is God who does the unfolding, not you. All you have to do is surrender your will to Him, align yourself to what He is doing and walk in it.

God doesn't always give us the full picture, maybe so as not to scare us with how BIG His plans are for us. Also, I believe it is because He wants to give us a chance to develop our faith in Him and build our character to become more like Jesus. He desires for us to use the free will He has given us to go where He leads us.

You may be called to be a Doctor and then find out that you enjoy writing as well. Are those two related? Do they match? I don't know.

However, what I know is God can use your skills as a doctor to help 'the body' and your writing talent to encourage and save 'souls'. You catch my drift?

It doesn't matter if your life callings, gifts and talents seem to match or appear unrelated, humanly speaking. In the eyes of God, the master planner, they all point towards one goal, which is to redeem lost souls back to Him. Nothing in your life is wasted with God and He can use it all if you allow Him.

Women are powerful

Lack of confidence affects men and women generally. However, I believe women - especially mothers - are affected more. Women are powerful. The act of getting pregnant and birthing a baby into this world is such a powerful calling, but the enemy has succeeded in using this powerful act to undermine women, making them feel inadequate.

A lot of women go through a traumatic childbirth experience, pre/post-natal depression, loneliness, verbal abuse, emotional abuse, physical abuse, loss, and other traumatic experiences. The idea that they could be called to something greater than themselves seems far-fetched.

The enemy – Satan, is aware that you have a calling on your life, which ultimately is to restore mankind back to God. As a result, he puts all kinds of hindrances in your way, especially doubt, to stop you from heeding the call.

Sometimes it is from those messy traumatic experiences that a great message, our earthly calling, is birthed.

He may not stop you from getting saved or accepting the love of Jesus, but he has successfully stopped many from bearing lasting fruit i.e. showing others about the saving power of Jesus through their calling. The enemy has caused so many to doubt that they have been called, leading to lack of confidence to pursue what they know they should be doing.

What we don't realise as women, is that sometimes it is from those messy traumatic experiences that a great message, our earthly calling, is birthed.

The Bible already tells us in Romans 8:28 (NLT) that:

*"God causes **everything** to work together for the good of those who love God and are called according to His purpose for them."*

What I need you to remember as you keep reading this book, is that if you love God, He is orchestrating everything to work for your good because you are called according to His purpose.

7

What is confidence?

According to the dictionary, it is the *"quality of being certain of your abilities or of having trust in people, plans, or the future."*

For so long, we have tried to have confidence in our own abilities, but we always fall short. We have trusted other people, but they have disappointed us deeply. We have been hurt and betrayed. We have concluded that we don't have what it takes and we are not enough.

Society makes us believe we are enough, but we know deep down that we don't have what it takes and we are not enough.

However, I have good news.

John 15:5 (NASB) says:

"I am the vine, you are the branches; he who abides in Me and I in him, he bears much fruit, for apart from Me you can do nothing."

Without Jesus, we cannot heed the call; neither can we bear lasting fruit.

If our confidence is in God, if we partner with Him on a daily basis, then He is enough for us to live a fulfilled and excellent life.

As you read this book, I pray that you will hear God speak to you intimately and uniquely. I pray that He will not only confirm what you were created to do, but also take you on an adventure where you are empowered to partner with Him in your life.

Do not allow fear to stop you from exploring the options that God presents to you. It is time to slay doubt. It is time for you to confidently manifest God's calling on your life through Christ who gives you strength.

Reflection:

1. What has happened in my life that has impacted my confidence to step out?

2. How can I partner with God to bear lasting fruit?

CHAPTER 2

YOUR CALLING IS RELEVANT

D oubting that you have been called, often comes from thinking that you have nothing to offer, or that what you have to offer is not relevant.

The enemy will try to make you believe that who you are or what you have is of no importance, that what you do does not matter. He may even give you 'evidence' and tell you nobody finds what you have to share or offer useful.

Unfortunately, a lot of women have fallen into the trap of believing this lie from the enemy, and as a result they stay in their little corner living an average life, doing the barest minimum.

Some of the ladies I have mentored and coached have told me that for years they knew their God-given assignment but did nothing about it because they believed it would not make a difference, or that someone out there was already doing something similar. Therefore, they didn't see the point of doing what someone was already doing.

The truth is that God has a special purpose for every single one of us. Before we were born, Abba appointed something unique for you and I to do on earth. He designed us with everything we need to fulfill that unique assignment. We are not here to just take up space, marry, make money, buy houses, drive nice cars, and die.

No! We were born for much more! We were born to bring God glory by using the gifts, resources, and dreams He has given each of us. We play a unique part in His redemption story.

I heard this analogy recently from one of my mentors, more like a question: *"You need air, I need air. Have you ever been afraid that because we both need air, you will run out of air? No, this is because air is abundant and even with billions of people on the planet, we are all still breathing and not depriving anyone else of their own quota of air."*

Now imagine you and your friend are under the sea with your oxygen tanks, scuba diving. Suddenly your friend's oxygen tank has an issue, you are not so quick to share your oxygen with your friend because it is limited and at that point is now a precious commodity.

Same air but different scenarios.

When it comes to our calling, the abundance perspective must always prevail. There is enough to go around. As they say *"the sky is big enough for us to all fly in."*

In fact, as Jesus put it, the laborers are few, but the harvest is plenty. There are more people who need help than there are helpers. So you pulling back because someone else is already doing something similar to what God has called you to do is an injustice to mankind…an injustice to the nation God has assigned to you.

Have you noticed that even when you know more than one person offering a specific product or service, you tend to gravitate towards one particular person?

You drive a particular model of car out of all the different models available out there

You attend one church out of numerous churches

You love Nando's chicken even though there are several chicken restaurants out there

You shop at Zara & ASOS and not at Marks & Spencer or any other shop

Why?

That's because there is something about them that attracts you. It could be their value system, price, style; whatever it is, you connected with them and you are now loyal to them.

That is the same with your God-given calling. The combination of your story, strengths, weaknesses, experiences, gifts, talents, personality, character, aura, gestures, failures, successes, quirkiness or lack of it makes you unique. Someone out there is attracted to your uniqueness.

It doesn't matter if a million people are already doing what you have been called to do. Your nation can feel your absence and are eagerly waiting for you to help them because of the uniqueness you have.

Even the Bible shows us clear examples of people who were called and 'nations' they were called to help:

Moses was called to lead the Israelites out of Egypt.
Esther was called to deliver the Jews from genocide.
Paul was called to preach the gospel of Jesus to the Gentiles.
Jesus was first called to the Jews and then the Gentiles.

This applies to us as well:

Pastors have different callings.
Doctors, counselors, professionals have different specialties.
Coaches have different groups of people they help.
Restaurants have different cuisines.
Hair salons have different hair types they cater to.

And so on and so forth.

> *Every morning say to yourself: "My calling is relevant, someone out there needs me"*

Do you see how important and relevant you are? I am not trying to flatter you, but to make you understand that you are significant because God deposited something unique in you.

You are relevant.

The dreams God has deposited in you, your gifts and talents are vital. That calling Abba keeps whispering into your heart is for the benefit of someone else.

The devil knows this and his job is to steal this calling from you. He wants to destroy it by putting doubt and lies in your head to make you stop what you are doing.

You cannot allow the enemy to steal your calling. Every morning say to yourself: *"My calling is relevant, someone out there needs me"* and receive boldness to be a blessing to someone that day.

How to stand out in a noisy world

Another excuse I hear from women is that when they finally do step out, no one is commending or applauding them.

They blog and no one comments on their blog posts.

They put up an encouraging post on Facebook and they only get a few likes and no comments.

They put up a video on YouTube but no one acknowledges it.

They advertise their products and services, only friends and family buy.

They write a book and only a handful of people buy a copy.

Yes, I have been there and know how painful this can be. It can feel demoralising not to have anyone applaud you when you step out to do what God has called you to do. Sometimes you may even face opposition, or you may not get any support, and it is so tempting to crawl back into the hole you came out from.

Before you crawl back into that hole, I want you to remember something. It was Abba who gave you the calling and not any human being. Therefore, your goal really should be to please your Heavenly father and not man. As hard as it may sound, even if no one acknowledges you or gives you feedback, as long as God told you to do something, keep doing it. Don't get distracted by the applause of others or lack of it. Just stay focused.

When you begin to make a difference, the right people - your nation - will begin to notice.

Let's face it, we live in a noisy, busy, fast paced environment where everyone is wrapped up in their little bubble and seems to have a short attention span.

How then can you stand out in a crowded noisy world? How do you get heard? *"Why should someone pay attention to me out of numerous people out there with a similar calling to me?"*

The answer points back to focusing on the nation God has called you to help. Build credibility and a relationship with them. The truth is not everyone can hear you. Your time and resources are limited, so you have to focus on using 80% of your time and resources on the 20% of people that need what you have. Speak to them directly and ignore everyone else.

As your nation begins to see the impact you bring, they will notice you and connect with you. Some might not acknowledge you publicly but trust me; they are being impacted by you.

I have experienced this personally. Some of the women I coach and mentor today, have followed me silently for years and when it was the right time, they reached out and connected with me. I then found out later that they had been listening to me and observing what I was doing for years.

The truth is some people in your nation will connect with you the first time they meet you. Some others need time to trust you, to know if you are the real deal and that you won't leave them hanging.

This is where consistency comes in on your part:

Show up day in day out without fail.
Choose calling over comfort.
Give value and provide solutions to the people who need it.

At the appointed time, the people in your nation will follow you. So don't worry that no one is publicly applauding you. Your Abba Father is happy and proud of you and that is what truly matters: Your audience of ONE.

My online program Digital Transformation for Super Working Mums[1] *amongst other things extensively teaches on how to find and attract your nation. It shows you how to serve your nation and solve their problems. Details for this program can be found in the appendix.*

Reflection:

1. What has God told me to do that I think is irrelevant?

2. How can I stand out in a noisy world?

CHAPTER 3

WHERE HAVE YOU BEEN CALLED TO SERVE?

The word 'calling' sometimes imply becoming a pastor or having a full-time ministry. This is not so. Every child of God has been called to influence a *sphere of society*, to bring transformation through the gospel of Jesus Christ.

The *Spheres of Society* are also referred to as the *Seven Mountains of Influence.*[2] In 1975 Bill Bright, founder of *Campus Crusade*, and Loren Cunningham, founder of *Youth With a Mission* received similar visions from God; that to influence any nation for Jesus Christ, we would have to penetrate the seven spheres or mountains that are the pillars of any society.

There is a particular mountain or in simpler terms, a particular sphere of society that God wants you to penetrate and influence.

Your assignment, the problem that you are called to solve, may fall into one or more of these mountains of influence or spheres of society. As you go through the seven spheres of society below, I would like you to begin to identify and reaffirm the area you have been called to serve in and influence for the Kingdom of God.

1. **Business**: called to create wealth in the marketplace with integrity and leadership. The income generated from businesses can fund other areas of influence.

2. **Arts and Entertainment**: called to reflect God's glory in arts, music, sports, fashion, and entertainment.

3. **Education**: called to bring transformational change to the educational system that serves us and particularly our children.

4. **Government**: called to positively affect all aspects of government through politics, governmental appointments, and policy making.

5. **Media**: called to bring light, encouragement and the gospel of Jesus Christ through news sources such as TV, social media (e.g. Facebook, Twitter, Instagram), blogs, podcasts, online videos, newspapers, radio, etc.

6. **Religion**: called to show people that Jesus is the way, how to develop an intimate relationship with God, and how to experience His presence and power in their lives.

7. **Families**: called to bring healing to the family unit, marriages, and other relationships within the family unit. Restoring Christ back to His rightful position as the head of the family.

Simple Case Studies

To illustrate the concept of spheres of society, I have provided a few examples of women in the *Super Working Mum Academy* who are influencing their spheres of society:

a. Lady F uses her skills and talents in three areas i) Arts and Entertainment, ii) Business and iii) Religion. She is gifted in graphics and design; she uses her gift of encouragement to inspire women through her inspirational greeting cards and home decor inscribed with encouraging Christian words. The proceeds from the greeting cards go to charity. Her business has helped a number of women design book covers, journals and branding for their businesses.

b. Lady Y is making waves in two areas: i) Education and ii) Family. She is a fertility nurse specialist who is passionate about helping couples that have difficulty conceiving, get pregnant. Apart from working in the National Health Service (NHS), she launched an organisation to educate women in ethnic minority communities and help them with the process of conceiving babies.

c. Lady B is passionate about bringing change to two areas i) Family and ii) Education. She runs a ministry that provides practical resources and tips to help teenage boys discover who they are, understand their purpose, boldly pursue their goals in life and become responsible men.

d. Lady D is a change agent in three areas i) Government, ii) Education and iii) Family. She champions the National Antibiotic Awareness campaign in the UK, educating families and healthcare professionals on how to use antibiotics appropriately. Over 30,000 people in the UK have signed up to be a part of creating awareness on using antibiotics only when necessary. We will hear more about her story later in the book.

I am so proud of what these women are doing to influence the areas they have been called to.

Some have been called to influence thousands, while some have been called to influence the one who will influence millions.

Now again you might be reading this thinking: "*All of these examples are of women who are out there influencing groups of people, but I am at home stuck with my children. Anytime I try to venture out, because that is what I see other women doing, I feel God pulling me back to stay at home and invest in my children.*"

We have all been called to different paths; some have been called to influence thousands, while some have been called to influence the one who will influence millions.

18

It is not about the number of people you are called to, but about recognising your calling and your area of influence. So if you are at home with your children, your area of influence is likely i) Education and ii) Family; training your children to fully possess their own area of influence, who in turn will influence a larger number of people.

The enemy has attacked and will continue to attack all of these areas. He has polluted the media, government, families, educational system, arts and entertainment industries, businesses and the church.

Matthew 9:37(NKJV) say *"The harvest truly is plentiful, but the labourers are few."*

We cannot afford to make any more excuses because our generation is depending on us. Our children's generation and the future generations are depending on us to partner with heaven. It is time for the daughters of Zion to arise and take their place. It is time to influence and bring God's light to the areas where you have been called to effect change for the Kingdom of God.

Reflection:

1. What mountain(s) have I been called to influence? Think of areas where you shine and where solutions come easily to you. That might just be your mountain of influence.

Action step:

1. Whatever your mountain of influence is, ask God to help you influence that area for His glory & His agenda and not yours.

CHAPTER 4

GOD CHOSE YOU

Slaying doubt and confidently manifesting God's calling on your life is about remembering that it was God who chose you and not the other way round.

It was God who put the desire in your heart to help a specific group of people. You waking up in the middle of the night thinking of how to help orphans, widows, the oppressed, the abused, the depressed, how to help organisations grow, or a set of people with a specific problem, was not your idea. It was God who put that passion in you.

Your calling feeds into God's agenda...
Your calling fits into a bigger picture...
Your calling is bigger than you...
Your calling is not about you...
Your calling is about what God wants to achieve on this earth...
Your calling is about declaring God's greatness on the earth...

The moment you make God's calling all about you, you become distracted, burdened, overwhelmed and resentful. The day you start to think God's calling on your life was your idea, is the day frustration comes knocking on your door and a dent in your confidence could occur.

I like how John 15:16 (NLT) puts it:

"You didn't choose me. I chose you. I appointed you to go and produce lasting fruit, so that the Father will give you whatever you ask for, using my name."

God appointed you to carry out a unique assignment. To produce lasting fruit, you will always need to rely on God and remember He chose you. Jesus also promises that whatever we ask for in His name, Abba Father will give to us.

When God called you, He designed you to be able to handle the challenges and victories that come with your unique assignment. So anytime you feel burdened or confused about how to walk in your calling, run back to the originator of the assignment. This could be at your job, business, in your marriage or as a parent.

Sometimes we lose our confidence because we have put our trust in other men or even in our own intellect to perform our calling. This could be occasions where God has asked you to create a new product and only a handful of people are buying it, or He asks you to write a book and no one seems interested, or maybe He gives you a new idea to pitch to your boss at work and it falls through.

God's agenda cannot be achieved by your intellect; it requires the supernatural help of Holy Spirit.

John 15:16 as mentioned above, is a key to what you need to do if you feel confused: ask God to impress upon your nation's minds your product, your book or whatever it is He has appointed you to create and see the supernatural step in.

God's agenda cannot be achieved by your intellect; it requires the supernatural help of Holy Spirit.

The role of Holy Spirit

So many books have been written about Holy Spirit and His role in our lives, so I won't go into much detail here. The focus in this book is on how Holy Spirit partners with you in carrying out your assignment. At the end of this chapter, I have provided the names of a few books you can read for more in-depth teaching about Holy Spirit.

Holy Spirit has been sent to help us live a purposeful life. In the book of John 14:26 (AMP), Jesus said this to His disciples:

"But the Helper (Comforter, Advocate, Intercessor-Counselor, Strengthener, Standby), the Holy Spirit, whom the Father will send in My name [in My place, to represent Me and act on My behalf], He will teach you all things. And He will help you remember everything that I have told you."

As we intentionally walk in purpose, so many things will come against us. Nevertheless, Holy Spirit is ever available to comfort us, counsel us, strengthen us, fight for us, defend us, intercede for us, teach us and help us navigate this broken world we live in.

I always say to the women I mentor and coach, Holy Spirit is your first mentor and coach. He wants to help you with ALL things. All means all, everything! Holy Spirit may instruct you to go to someone to mentor or coach you in aspects of your calling, but ultimately, He is your first port of call.

You are not likely to know every aspect of your calling and by trying to figure it all out by yourself, you are likely to go off course or waste time. However, with the help of Holy Spirit, who knows everything about you and your calling, He will begin to direct you, open doors for you and connect you with people that will propel you to the next level.

I have had situations where I have been stuck on the next line of action to take but as soon as I asked Holy Spirit to help me, I heard Him whisper solutions to me. I've heard Him say, *"call this person"*, or *"post this message on Facebook"* or do this or do that and boom! I see the results.

Holy Spirit wants to be a part of everything you do, even your social media posts, if you let Him.

I remember one time when the sales of the *Living Amazed Journal* dwindled. I was getting discouraged and I wondered why no one was buying this amazing journal that a lot of other women had testified was a blessing to them. My confidence was waning as well. So I took it to God in prayer for a new strategy on how to get the journal into the hands of those who needed it. I remember at the beginning of the New Year in 2017, I shared with God the number of journals I would like to sell that month. I also asked Holy Spirit for a strategy on how to reach those who needed the journal.

Holy Spirit gave me two strategies: one was to write a blog post series on the benefit of journaling, and the second was to share the journal with the ladies in my local church following our Pastor's recommendation at the watch night service that we must get a journal for the new year. I was not at the service, but I listened to the recording and felt the Lord saying to share about the *Living Amazed Journal*. I hesitated initially but I knew that if I wanted a breakthrough I had to obey. So I did my part: I wrote some blog posts and told the ladies in my church about the journal on our WhatsApp group.

Before I knew it, online orders starting coming in - one copy here, two copies there, five copies here, I was astonished! To crown it all, one of the ladies who bought a journal is part of the church executive and she showed our Pastor the *Living Amazed Journal*. He loved it. On two Sundays in a row, my Pastor showcased the journal during church service. As a result, I was able to sell more journals, which exceeded the number of journals I had written down at the beginning of the month.

One thing that struck me when my Pastor talked about the *Living Amazed Journal* at church was this: *"This journal was prepared ahead of time for you (the audience)."*

Sometimes when God appoints us to create something to sell, the sales might not come immediately. It doesn't mean you didn't hear right. This is not the time to feel dejected but to get yourself prepared. It is usually a matter of timing. The way Holy Spirit works is totally different from the way the world works. At the right time, Holy Spirit will give you a strategy to put your product, service or idea out there and the right people who need it will buy what you have to offer.

To confidently manifest God's calling, you have to surrender completely to Holy Spirit and not try to do it your way or the way of the world.

The way of the world is to:

strive and hustle,
work round the clock,
not have time for family or what is important because they want to
make ends meet.

Our desire should be to emulate Peter who immediately obeyed when Jesus told him to cast his net on the other side of the boat, and he then caught a multitude of fish.

When you partner with Holy Spirit you will catch a great harvest. You will see results in your business, ministry, job or wherever you have been called to serve.

Dynamis

Acts 1:8 (NIV) say: *"But you will receive power when the Holy Spirit comes on you; and you will be my witnesses in Jerusalem and in all Judea and Samaria, and to the ends of the earth."*

The word power here is the Greek word *'dynamis'*. This means *strength, power, ability, mighty work, power for performing miracles, the power and influence, which belong to riches and wealth, moral power and excellence of soul.*

This is the kind of power Jesus promised to the disciples and every child of God when we partner and align our spirit to Holy Spirit.

Dynamis was the same power that overshadowed Mary who conceived our Lord Jesus supernaturally. *Dynamis* was the same power that raised Jesus from the dead.

Why is this type of power required?

Because we need power beyond our natural abilities, to do what we have been commissioned to do. Remember, your calling is tied to God's agenda, which is ultimately to win souls for the Kingdom of God. This cannot be done in your own strength or intellect. It is so important that you walk in *dynamis* to achieve mighty things in your calling.

The devil isn't happy that you want to walk in your calling so he will do all he can to:

stop you,
destroy or abort your dreams,
steal your joy.

So you need d*ynamis,* wonder-working power, to stir up your gifts and to oppose the enemy when he comes with his lies and distractions.

You need *dynamis* to rise above criticism, disappointments, malicious behaviour, lack of resources, and anything else that will come against you to deter you from focusing on achieving God's purpose for your life.

Dynamis is not like worldly power, which wants to manipulate or control others, or make another human being depend solely on one. Holy Spirit power is available to subdue the flesh, so that He might remold us and build our character.

How do you activate *dynamis?*

Dynamis is available to every believer of God. However, we have to activate this power in our lives. It's like a building that has electricity but until the light is switched on, the electric power is dormant.

We need to *'switch the light on'* so that power can flow through us. We can activate *dynamis* by:

Humbly acknowledging our helplessness and our complete dependence on God: This power can only be manifested in a life that is totally submitted to God's will. By admitting our weakness and that we need help, yielding our thoughts, desires, and will to Holy Spirit daily, His power can flow through us.

Studying the word of God: F. F. Bosworth said, *"Most Christians feed their body three hot meals a day and their spirit one cold snack a week. And they wonder why they're so weak in faith."* To walk in *dynamis* we must study the word of God daily so that our spirit man has the capacity to receive and handle the things of the Spirit. Also, Holy Spirit is able to flow unhindered through our spirit to our soul and then to our body where we live out our calling. When our spirit, soul and body are in alignment and one with Holy Spirit, His power can flow through us effortlessly.

Meditation: Not only should we study God's word; we must take it a step further by meditating on the word of God, which Holy Spirit can quicken in our lives. Some people get confused when they hear the word *'meditate'*. It basically means to go over something again and again in your mind. We all meditate, but the question is what are you meditating on? When you worry you are meditating, when you rehash a problem in your mind you are meditating, but we want to flip that over. Instead of rehashing your problem, ruminate on the word of God; ponder on what God says about that situation. Holy Spirit is able to work with the word of God in your heart so that it becomes a reality in your life.

By stepping out in faith and boldness when Holy Spirit gives us simple instructions on what to do, more power flows through us. With time we will begin to do greater works through *dynamis* like Jesus promised.[1]

Doubt and fear have no place to stay when the Holy Spirit is in charge of our affairs.

Further study on the Holy Spirit

1. *Holy Spirit My Senior Partner* by David Yonggi Cho
2. *Good Morning, Holy Spirit* by Benny Hinn
3. *How You Can Be Led by the Spirit of God* by Kenneth E Hagin

Reflection:

1. How can I activate dynamis in my life today?

Action step:

1. Acknowledge the areas were you are weak; feel helpless or stuck in your calling. Ask Holy Spirit for wisdom on what to do.

CHAPTER 5

INVEST IN YOUR CALLING

O ne reason why many women get frustrated as they heed the calling of God is that they are expecting too much to happen so soon. God has given them this big dream and they try to rush ahead of God, expecting their big dream to manifest immediately. When it doesn't happen as expected, they get worked up, lose their confidence, start to doubt, then abandon the process and wonder if they were truly called.

One counsel I always give the women I mentor and coach is this: **Dream BIG but start SMALL**. Start with what you have and where you are. Do not allow a lack of resources or not having the full picture overwhelm you.

Place your big vision in front of you but take baby action steps. Stop sitting around waiting for the big break to come. Get to work. Be faithful with the little God has given you now, and then He will begin to open more doors of opportunity.

Luke 16:10 (NLT) say: *"If you are faithful in little things, you will be faithful in large ones. But if you are dishonest in little things, you won't be honest with greater responsibilities."*

Even if God's purpose for you is to be the CEO of a multinational company, he will not give you such a huge responsibility from day one. He will start you off from the basics, so as to build your character.

I have heard of CEOs of companies who start off their children from the bottom of the ladder. These kids move up from one department to the other, learning the operations of each department until they eventually get to the top. By doing this, they know the ins and outs of their father's company, gain confidence and also develop character along the way. Imagine if these children were made CEO from day one; that would probably be the beginning of the end of that company.

Dream BIG but start SMALL

This also applies to us in the Kingdom of God.

Isn't it amazing that God doesn't give us more responsibility than we can handle? If He did, we would probably collapse under so much pressure. He brings small opportunities our way and expects us to handle them faithfully and wisely. As we do this and He sees our obedience, faithfulness, and maturity, He will begin to bring bigger opportunities our way.

Invest in yourself

Many of us are waiting on God to do something, but God is waiting on us to prepare for the journey ahead. We do this by investing in ourselves.

What does it mean to invest in yourself? It means to educate yourself continually, especially in the areas of personal growth, your skills and your craft. I don't necessarily mean going back to school but developing skills that will boost your confidence and expertise in life and business. The day you stop investing in yourself is the day you begin to die.

If you don't invest in yourself, no one else will, and the truth is most people will only invest their time and resources in you when they see that you are investing in yourself. You don't have to announce that you are investing in yourself. It will show in your habits, in your words and in your actions. As you grow it will reflect in your life and how you handle situations.

If you are a singer, you can invest in vocal coaching to train your voice.

If you love to write, write regularly. You can also invest in writing classes.

If you love to speak, use every opportunity given to speak. You can also invest in public speaking classes.

If you have a business, get some marketing help. Get a coach or a mentor.

In your career, invest in your personal development

The list goes on and on...

A lot of women find it easier to invest in (buy) material things but when it comes to their personal development, they wing it or justify why they shouldn't spend money on their growth. You have to be intentional about your personal growth.

When you invest in yourself it affects everything else you do for the better. You become a better wife, better parent, better manager of your finances, better business owner, better employee etc. Also, your worth increases. You become more confident in yourself and in your abilities.

When I started *Super Working Mum* (SWM), I didn't know what I was doing. I had a mandate from God, but I didn't know the steps to take to manifest the vision. I knew I could write, so I started with the skill I had. I wrote on the SWM blog for mothers but didn't know what else to do with the blog, but I kept writing. For a whole year, I followed all kinds of free advice online on how to monetise the blog. I made several mistakes while praying hard but alas I didn't move forward. I was frustrated but thankfully I didn't give up. Then it happened! I was three months pregnant with my son, when I lost my job. That was a very dark period for my family and I, as my husband had also been out of work for some time, but it was also the push I needed to take proper action.

31

I took the leap of faith and prayerfully joined a paid business coaching group I found on Facebook. It was just £10 a month to subscribe but a very big step for me especially as I had just lost my job and my husband was out of work. However, for the first time ever, I took a risk and invested money to grow *Super Working Mum*. Surprisingly, what I had tried to do by myself in 12 months, I accomplished in 3 months! My eyes were opened to another world I never knew existed. In this group, I learnt how to set up a proper business online and how to grow a business mindset.

That same year, I also got my first ten clients. I later hired my own coach and my business really skyrocketed from there. By God's grace, SWM has expanded (and is still expanding) into speaking engagements, coaching & mentoring women through the *Super Working Mum Academy*, online programs, weekend retreats, creating journals and writing books. I have grown spiritually and emotionally.

I now prioritise my personal growth because as I grow, I can pour into others. As I grow, more God-given ideas come to me to implement. As I improve, I give more value to the nation God has assigned to me. As I grow, I make God proud.

Ways to invest in yourself

1. **Read and Listen**: Read the Bible, it has all the success strategies you will ever need. Read other books relevant to you. This is probably one of the easiest ways to invest in yourself without breaking the bank. Invest in audio books that you can listen to on the go if you don't have time to sit down and read. Listen to edifying podcasts or sermons as you drive, or travel on the plane, train or bus.

2. **Take care of you**: It is IMPORTANT that you take care of you because until you take care of you, you cannot really take care of others. Eat energy boosting foods, such as oranges, bananas, almonds, oats, broccoli, spinach, green smoothies etc. Eliminate junk food and take supplements. Drink lots of water, sleep well

and exercise. Engage in activities that make you relax and happy. Go on a retreat or spa break with other women!

3. **Get a mentor or a coach**: Not everything you find online is reliable, besides it can take longer to manifest your dreams if you have no help. Prayerfully look for someone who has gone ahead of you and can show you how to do things quicker and with less hassle. One of the prices a mentor or coach pays is going the longer route and making some mistakes, so that you won't have to do the same. They do all the groundwork and can show you step by step how to execute quicker and faster, breaking things down in ways you can assimilate easily. Time is of the essence here. This step is likely going to involve you investing money, and most people run away from this because they think hiring a coach or mentor is expensive. What is expensive is wasting years trying to figure it out by yourself. You are sowing into your future when you invest financially into your growth.

In summary, don't get hung up about the big vision. Take small steps every day to manifest your BIG dreams, invest in your growth and prayerfully invest in a mentor or coach. If investing in a coach is expensive for you, then you can start off with a monthly mentoring support group such as the *Super Working Mum Academy*[3]. There are definitely many mentoring groups available, so do some research to find a community that would suit your needs. This could be an online group or one in your local vicinity that allows for more face-to-face interactions.

You will begin to see transformation in your life as you invest in your growth.

Reflections:

1. What small steps can I take every day to make my dream a reality?

2. In what ways can I start investing in myself?

3. What would I need to sacrifice to make that happen?

NAVIGATING THE SEASONS OF YOUR LIFE

In the next section of this book, we are going to look at three seasons of life that could potentially hinder you from walking freely in God's calling on your life. These three seasons could cause you to doubt your calling, affect your confidence and stop you from bearing lasting fruit.

When it comes to God's calling on your life, the enemy is after one thing: your fruitfulness. He can't touch God's love for you, but he can derail you with life's issues, doubt, insecurities, self-ambition, jealousy, comparison, anger, bitterness, laziness, evil communication, etc. These, in turn, can impact your fruitfulness, that is, your ability to impact your nation and transform lives.

Remember God's purpose is to restore mankind back to Himself, and He needs you and I to fulfill this purpose. God needs an army that will break people free from bondage and captivity. We cannot allow the enemy to get in the way.

We shall explore how to confidently manifest God's calling on your life, no matter what season of life you may be going through. As you read the next section, you might find yourself in one particular season or a combination of all the three seasons. I hope the strategies and stories shared will help you come up with an action plan to press through each season.

These seasons are Your Past, Your Preparation and Your Project.

SECTION 2

CHAPTER 6

NAVIGATING YOUR PAST

I would like to use the story of Esther in the Bible, to illustrate and delve more into how you can confidently manifest God's calling on your life whilst navigating your past.

Esther had a past before she became queen. Esther was an orphan raised by her Uncle Mordecai. I am sure that she must have felt lonely, awkward, different and maybe even insignificant, as a child.

There is no mention in the Bible of Esther having any siblings, so it appears it was just her and her uncle, who was her guardian and mentor.

This must have been tough for Esther, as she had experienced loss and grief at a young age. Just when she thought life was getting a bit better, she was forcefully taken away from her dear uncle - the only family she had - into the King's palace simply because the King was looking for a new bride. What horror!

It was as if all Esther had in her life was loss after loss. Again, she must have wondered why this was happening to her; losing everyone she loved. I imagined that she would have cried and gotten angry, wondering why her life wasn't perfect. But guess what, even though she didn't know this at the time (and remember we only know what happened at the end of her life because we have read the full story in the Bible), her past was preparing her for her special chosen assignment.

What is your life story? What have you gone through in the past or what are you going through now that is causing you pain? What are those defining moments in your life?

I want you to know that everything that has happened in your life up to this very point: the good, the bad and the ugly, even the fact that you are reading this book, is for a reason.

As mentioned earlier in Chapter 1, Romans 8:28 says, *"everything works together for the good of those who love God."* Note that this promise was not given to everyone. This promise is only for those who love God and have been chosen, that is, elected, selected according to HIS purpose.

> *God allows in His wisdom what He could easily prevent by His power."*

You are not your past, nevertheless, do not discount what happened in your past: the rape, the sexual abuse, the bullying, the loss of a dear one, or the divorce. Whatever pain you have experienced in your past, God wants to use it for good if you give Him your pain.

Please note that I am not saying God caused your pain, yes, He knew about it and allowed it to happen. Graham Cooke, a minister of God I love, once said: *"God allows in His wisdom what He could easily prevent by His power."*

God is powerful and could have prevented that bad thing from happening to you but in His wisdom, He chose not to intervene for a bigger reason beyond you.

We live in a fallen world where bad things happen. God never promised us that our lives would be easy, but He promised to always be there with us. He wants to turn your pain around for your good and for His glory, if you will let him.

When I was young, my dad's cousin who lived with us sexually abused me. I didn't share this with anyone for a long time, as I felt ashamed and that somehow it was my fault. It was a bad thing that happened to me, but now I understand why I am passionate and compassionate towards women and the girl child.

Forgiving my uncle was one of the hardest things to do, but I realised I had carried the pain and bitterness with me for a long time. There was a limit to how far I could go in life with the trauma I was carrying. I had to remind myself over and over again that I forgave him for myself; so that I could be set free in my mind to walk in my calling, and so I could have a better and more intimate relationship with my husband. I also had to forgive my parents, as subconsciously I was angry with them for not protecting me from the abuse. Of course, they were not aware but the little girl in me expected them to know.

You may have experienced defining moments, both positive and negative, that have shaped your life in significant ways. You may have stopped yourself from truly living because of something traumatic that happened in your past and in the bid to protect yourself from further hurt.

I want you to begin to see your past from a different perspective - God's perspective. I want you to clearly see how God has been at work in every area of your life. I want you to notice where you have stopped yourself from living to your full potential because of what happened in your past.

Reflecting on your past may also reveal to you the people you need to forgive (*including yourself*) so that you can move forward confidently in your calling. The journey of forgiveness can be a painful one, but Christ has given us the grace and ability to forgive.

You may have to go through a process of forgiveness as I did, but remember Holy Spirit is with you and will show you what you need to do at each point. The book *Grace and Forgiveness* by John and Carol Arnott[4] is a book I will recommend to you if you need to walk through this process.

Until you completely embrace your past and forgive those who hurt you, it is unlikely that you will be able to confidently walk in your calling.

Reflections:

Think of your past: the life changing, defining moments in your life.

1. What lessons have I learnt?

2. How is my life different?

3. How am I different?

4. Where have I stopped myself from moving forward?

5. Where have I taken a leap of faith to move forward in my life?

6. Who in my past/present do I need to forgive?

Action step:

1. Write a letter to the person(s) you need to forgive, pour out your heart and tell them they owe you nothing and that you forgive them. Then tear up the letter.

2. If you need to walk through the forgiveness process then get the book Grace and Forgiveness, which I recommended earlier (see end notes for details).

FROM TRIPPING TO TRANSFORMATION

Story 1

Here is the story of a lady who has successfully navigated her past and is positively impacting others:

I am Coach Toyin, Christian Transformation Coach and Founder of an online platform called *The Narrow Gateway*. My passion is twofold; one, to help Christians to identify and break free from blockages that prevent them from experiencing *'the glorious God-life'* of living supernaturally, living in intimacy with God and living out their God-given purpose. Closely related to this is my second passion, which is that through my work, I introduce Christians to the complete truth of the Gospel of the Kingdom of God, because even the most well-meaning Christian is stuck with a pale *'God-life'* if he/she has only been exposed to an incomplete version of the Gospel.

How the journey began

In February 2017, God not only gave me the specific title, *"Christian Transformation Coach"*, but He also gave me clear (not to mention dramatic) instructions on what my work would be, going forward. Receiving this kind of clarity about my God-given purpose was one of the most exhilarating experiences of my life. *"Me? Oluwatoyin?"*

You see, as a child, I had vivid visions of myself, microphone in hand, standing on a raised platform in a massive arena with lots of flashing lights. Whether I was singing or speaking, my message to the people in the arena was always about Christ.

I was raised in a Christian family and when I was a baby, my parents asked God for a word for my life. He gave them Psalm 34:1, which says *"I will exalt the Lord at all times, His praise shall continually be on my lips."* So you see, I grew up knowing that verse to be my identity, and I believed that my life purpose was to testify loudly to the world about Jesus Christ.

That perfect picture of my God-given purpose began shattering in my mid-teens when I *'tripped and fell'*; I began filling my heart's crevices with counterfeit love and acceptance. I backslid so badly that when I returned to Christ after a few years, I saw no path to freedom from the lifestyle of sin and brokenness that I had fallen into.

Worst of all, the shame of my past blunders shrouded me; condemnation and
guilt convinced me that those childhood dreams that I would one day stand on a platform and testify about Jesus were actually *'childish dreams'*. How could I even begin to consider fulfilling an assignment to testify about Jesus, when my back-story was so colourful, and when I had not yet fully broken free from old habits?

But God set me up and set me free! Hallelujah! He used my very struggles with guilt, habitual sin and brokenness to unsettle me such that I began to demand for *'the real God-life'*. I began to demand that since I was now restored to my relationship with God, I MUST walk in freedom from sin and inner brokenness, I MUST hear God's voice and walk in His purpose for my life, my life MUST be marked by God's supernatural power that shifts impossible situations.

My unsettledness made room for God to set me on a transformation journey, and though that journey is still ongoing today, somewhere along the way, the Lord began spotlighting my childhood dreams and reigniting my abandoned passions.

He showed me that through the *'roots and routes'* that my life had taken, He had fitted me with the tools that I would use to fulfil that very childhood vision that had thus far eluded me. WOW!!! Basically, my life had filled in the blanks to my God-given assignment, and I was now *'ready to rumble'*.

I must mention Detola Amure and the *Super Working Mum Academy* (SWMA) at this point, because they are one of the strategic contributors to my being equipped to step out into my calling. You see, when the Lord was igniting me, I knew Detola (we were childhood friends) and I knew about SWMA, but I really did not feel like joining a ladies' group online. However, the Lord specifically instructed me to join SWMA, and when I obeyed, I met like-minded women who were also battling giants standing between them and their calling. These women, like myself, were winning the war against mediocre living and through constructive interactions with them on SWMA, I gained strength and support to stick to my purpose-driven path.

Facing resistance

Life after stepping out into my God-given calling was not all sunshine and roses. Within the first couple of months, I crashed into the enemy's resistance. It manifested itself in repeated (not to mention bizarre) obstacles to my process of setting up my platform, fear, loneliness in ministry and embarrassment. I felt folks were mocking me for leaving a lucrative job and career for a *'fly by night'* occupation (I am a corporate lawyer by profession and before stepping out into my calling, I had had about 12 years of legal practice experience in top African and international institutions).

I also faced the reality that I had not come into ministry with family connections, ministry connections, money or anything that would springboard my work. I was literally starting with nothing and building my platform from the ground up.

I can't describe the emotional and spiritual effort, not to mention the financial cost that this takes. Yet, God's clear instruction to me was/is that I should faithfully set up the platform and framework for the ministry and I should minister to Him as my audience of One, and trust that in His time, He would bring the *'human audience'*.

I have been ready to give up about three times. Each time, the Lord would say to me, *"Who told you that you can give up? Have you done what I instructed you to do?"* And then He would encourage my spirit to trust Him and just obey. During this time, the Lord has twice instructed me to down tools and rest, and when I wanted to disobey, He blocked my attempts to keep working, until I finally gave in and obeyed.

The most recent time that I told the Lord that I was quitting, I was heavily pregnant with my third child. The Lord asked me yet again if I had done what He instructed me to do. I said, *"No"*. He then supernaturally introduced me to a content manager, and though she only worked with me for about two months, she breathed such new life and growth into my platform that folks were asking me how I had managed to re-launch my platform at the same time when I was giving birth to a third child! Well, my answer is, *"Oluwadabira";* the Lord has worked a wonder (which, by the way is my daughter's name).

Let me pull this all together by saying this: There is nothing better than a life lived within your God-given assignment. There is no obstacle, no matter how formidable, that is worth losing out on a purpose-driven life for. Your nation is waiting for you to rise and rule. Your mountain is waiting for you to climb and conquer. Your flock (nation) is waiting to hear and follow your voice. Creation is waiting in earnest expectation for the revelation of the children of God.

Transformative difference

Aside from experiencing God's approval for the work I do, the most rewarding part of this journey has been hearing from folks who through following my work and life, have been ignited into

44

their own transformation journey into *'the glorious God-life'*.

I have folks who had no clue of their God-given purpose but are now in the know and set up to step into their calling. I've even had folks who are not Christian contact me to say that my very public transformation process over the years has inspired them to intentionally pursue a purpose-driven life! Praise God!

If you are struggling to step out into your God-given assignment, my advice for you is this: fire up your passionate and consistent relationship with the Lord because your power to step out and stay within your God-given assignment comes from nowhere else.

God does not need you to be the most powerful Christian before you step out. He just needs you to be committed to a transformation journey with Him, and through your journey, He will tag on to you the tools you need and unravel off of you the fears and other giants that are vying for your purpose.

Understand that your heritage and right as a child of God is to live by every word that proceeds from the mouth of God.

Friend, you must stay so in tune with the Lord that you can hear His voice, and when you hear Him, live by it; trust Him and obey. This assignment you have is not going to be conquered by your human intellect and savvy.

Yes, you might be super brilliant and able to do a great job of it all on your own, but it will lack that supernatural edge that makes ALL OF THE TRANSFORMATIVE DIFFERENCE!

Will you be afraid to step out? Yes.

When you step out, will you face opposition? Oh yes!

Will you be just fine? Very much so, if you stay close to the Lord, listen for His instructions, and then trust & obey Him.

CHAPTER 7

ENJOY YOUR PREPARATION SEASON

A lmost everyone in the Bible who had a calling on his or her life had to go through a time of preparation. You name them: Moses, Joshua, Daniel, Samuel, Mary the mother of Jesus, John the Baptist, Paul, Peter, even Jesus.

Again, we will look into the life of Esther to see what lessons we can learn about embracing the preparation stage.

Your past, as we discussed in the previous chapter, is part of your preparation season. However, the kind of preparation we want to address in this chapter is what is happening in your life right now.

Following the story of Esther, after the King's officers at the King's decree took her, she was put in a place called a harem, with many other girls waiting to know what their fate would be. Because God chose Esther for an assignment bigger than herself, He was with her even in her time of confusion. She found favour with Hegai, the man who was in charge of all the girls.

Esther 2:9 (NASB) says:
"Now the young lady pleased him and found favor with him. So he quickly provided her with her cosmetics and food, gave her seven choice maids from the king's palace and transferred her and her maids to the best place in the harem."

When I read this passage, it made me wonder why it was only Esther that was recorded to have found favour with Hegai out of so many girls. There must have been something different about her.

Life in the harem would have been full of confusion, jealousy, fear and insecurities amongst the girls. I believe that if Esther had a nasty attitude; if she was always complaining, wearing a frown on her face and sulking, she won't have found favour with Hegai.

Yes, even though she was in pain and was confused, she did not allow her pain to cloud her mind. She was a delight to behold. She was obedient; she had a gentle and quiet spirit. She did everything Hegai and her uncle told her to do.

Now before we go further, I want you to notice something here. The King had a banquet in the third year of his reign[2], this was when his first wife Vashti refused to display her beauty to the King's guests and he got angry, sent her packing, and gave the command that all the girls of the land be brought to him.

Esther got to see the King in the 7th year of his reign[3]. So we can safely assume that Esther was in the harem for up to four years, with no family, undergoing intense preparation just to spend one night with the King. Within that time was also an intense 12-month beautification process.

Most of the girls there would have given up and *said "Well, the King will only choose one girl at the end of the day, I doubt it will be me, so let me live my life as I wish... I am already doomed anyway."*

We are limited more by our attitude than by opportunities.

But Esther did not behave like that. She didn't have her uncle with her anymore, but she had Hegai. She listened to Hegai and followed his advice on what to do as she prepared. There are some nuggets we can pick from Esther's life, to help you navigate your preparation season:

1. A solid attitude

It is said that we are limited more by our attitude than by opportunities. A positive mind attracts opportunities for success, while a negative mind repels them. Having a sour attitude, complaining all the time can delay you or can block you from confidently manifesting God's call on your life. Joyce Meyer once said, *"Enjoy where you are, on the way to where you are going."* She also said, *"Patience is not the ability to wait, but the ability to keep a good attitude while waiting."* Your attitude is very important to your success. It can lead you down the path of success or along the road of failure. Stay grateful.

2. Surround yourself with mentors.

I addressed this before briefly. Take advice from those who have walked the path or are more knowledgeable than you. If you can, have different mentors for different aspects of your life as led by Holy Spirit. Don't be a *'know it all'*.. Aim to learn something new every day. Esther's mentor was her Uncle Mordecai. It was recorded that she obeyed and listened to what her uncle taught her. Later on, Hegai became her mentor and she followed his instructions, which led to favour in the King's place.

Prayerfully begin to identify the *'Hegais'* and *'Mordecais'* God has put in your life. These are the people that will favour you and quickly come to your aid to show you the way. These are your destiny helpers. Don't despise them, instead appreciate them and invest in them. Learn as much as you can from them, for they have been put in your life to show you the way. And when you move on from a certain preparation stage, your mentors may change as well.

3. Know your seasons and adjust accordingly to change.

Being sensitive to the season you are in will go a long way toward confidently manifesting God's calling on your life. In winter, you would not dress like it is summer otherwise you might freeze to death. Likewise, you should be prepared to adjust according to the season of life you find yourself in. In Esther's case, Mordecai was no longer available to guide, nurture and protect her but God brought Hegai into her life. Esther could have remained stuck in the past, upset that her uncle was not around, but she realised things had changed and she quickly adjusted. The only thing constant in life is change, so be prepared for change.

Your wilderness experience

The wilderness experience is likely to be a big part of your preparation season. A lot of people shy away from having this experience because it can be a very lonely and painful place to be. I would like to put some emphasis on this aspect of your preparation season, because how you navigate this phase will either set you up for success or failure.

Moses grew up in a palace; therefore, he lived a very comfortable life initially. However, to be able to lead the children of Israel out of Egypt, he also had to live in the wilderness. The first 40 years of Moses' life in the palace were just as crucial as the 40 years he spent in the wilderness. He needed the mentality of a king to lead the children of Israel out of slavery, but he also needed the wilderness experience to build his character and to know what it felt like to not enjoy an affluent life. Every season of Moses' life mattered and helped him fulfill God's call on his life. Both the palace and the wilderness were preparation for what God had ultimately called Moses to do – to deliver the children of Israel from captivity.

Looking at the life of Jesus, when he was baptised by John the Baptist, a loud voice came from heaven saying: *"This is my beloved Son, in whom I am well-pleased."*

In essence, this was a public declaration of God's approval over

Jesus' calling. Following that, Jesus was led by the Spirit of God into the wilderness to be tempted by the devil.

The last thing you would expect after this public declaration was for Jesus to be led into the wilderness to be tempted by the devil. Why do we think Holy Spirit led Him into the wilderness? Because His character had to be tested.

Even though He was God, He left His power, title and everything that came with it and became a man so that He could experience what it meant to live as a man on earth. Jesus passed this test in the wilderness. This tells me that Jesus understands everything I may be going through. Jesus has gone through several temptations just like me and so He can relate. It wasn't just those three times he was tempted, as the Bible records that the devil left him till another opportune time.

What does the wilderness mean in the context of our calling? It means a time where we appear to have been deserted or abandoned by people. It means a time where we may experience rejection, loss, barrenness or darkness. A time where even though God is there, He appears to be silent.

The wilderness season is a time of character building, which comes either before we are commissioned to go out and manifest the big dreams God has placed in us, or before we are moved up to the next level of our calling.

It is a phase during which God takes our souls through a healing process. It could take different forms, e.g. purification like Esther's case, imprisonment like Joseph experienced, mockery and rejection like Nehemiah's situation, or temptation like Jesus went through in the wilderness.

You may have experienced
the loss of a job...
the loss of a home...
the loss of money...
the loss of friends...

living in a different country from your spouse and/or children...
separation or divorce from your spouse ...
chronic sickness and pain...
the death of a spouse or child...
ridicule from family and friends...
betrayal by a loved one...

Whatever it may be, as hard as it may be, this is not the time to wallow in self-pity. Instead, hand over your pain to Jesus, cling to Him and allow Him to work on your character and your heart. Sometimes it is only through pain and suffering that we realise how much of Jesus we need. It is during our time of hurt that we need more of Jesus and less of our flesh.

When you gave your life to Jesus, your spirit became born again. However, your soul has to go through a sanctification process. This is why the Bible says in Romans 12:2 that we should renew our minds through the word of God. If we are willing, the wilderness is a time to get our minds renewed and to develop our character and emotions.

It is because of the Kingdom that we are led into our wilderness experience. So that we can come out as pure as gold and with a heart totally surrendered to Jesus.

Most times our calling relates to people's lives; we need to go through some challenges to develop the confidence, and compassion needed to help the people God has called us to. We have to be careful when dealing with other people's lives; we cannot afford to help others when our emotions are still in a mess, because if we do, we are in danger of messing up people's lives. We have to come from a place of love and empathy to be able to transform lives.

If you have not experienced the loss of a child, how can you truly comfort a woman who has just lost a child?

If you have not experienced rejection, how can you truly encourage someone faced with rejection?

If you have not experienced separation from your spouse, how can you truly help someone experiencing the same?

Wisdom comes from a place of adversity.

This is not to say you cannot help someone going through a difficult time if you haven't been through similar difficulties. However, there is a big difference between when you have experienced what your nation is experiencing, and when you only have a theoretical knowledge of what they are experiencing. There is an authenticity that comes from having walked in their shoes and felt their pain; you are able to empathise and comfort others with the comfort God has given you because you know what it feels like and you can truly identify with them.

Like someone once said to me, wisdom comes from a place of adversity. Some of the dark times you have gone through are for the benefit of those coming behind you.

A few months ago (at the time of writing this book) I experienced the sudden death of my third child – my 7-month-old twin baby boy - Morakinyo Caleb. My life changed in an instant. I didn't see that coming and it shook me to my core. It shook my faith and made me question everything including if life was worth living. I was angry with God for allowing my son to die. Even though I am still very sad for my loss, I am now at a place of peace knowing my baby is in heaven. God permitted him to die as a baby; I may not understand why, but I know it is working for good and there is a bigger purpose for this very painful incident.

I am embracing my new normal and trusting God to see me through. I am still very much on the healing journey. By God's grace, I believe that at the right time my story of grieving and healing from the loss of my baby will help other women - especially women of colour - who may be experiencing similar pain.

When people talk about your life, will they talk about how you dealt with the challenges you faced, or will they talk about how you were consumed by the challenges? Will your life be a testament to God's faithfulness or not?

Do not rush your preparation period

This is probably the most crucial nugget of all. It took Esther many years to meet the King. She had to go through a beautification process, which lasted a year, and then she had to wait her turn before she could see the King. In total, it took her four years to spend just one night with the King. This was Esther's wilderness experience. Esther could have given up along the way, but she didn't. She stayed with the process even though it was hard.

It is likely that you are in your preparation stage. You are going through your beautification process...your wilderness experience. I checked up my concordance for the meaning of the word beautification used in this scripture and it means scraping or rubbing.

During your wilderness time, God is scraping or rubbing off some habits, some behaviours, and mindsets from you, so that you can take up the unique assignment He has called you to or to move you to the next level. He is purifying you daily; removing all the blemishes and hindrances, for the great work He has planned ahead for you.

Remember, your calling is bigger than you, and God will use anything to accomplish His purpose. So it will only make sense for you to be free of impediments that may impact on you completing your assignment.

There are negative mindsets and emotional baggage that you cannot afford to carry along with you on this journey of purpose. So Abba is stripping those weights away during your preparation season and also preparing you for the people He has called you to help. It can be a hard and gruesome process, but it is necessary for the Kingdom of God to be established.

Identify this season for what it is and take it in good stride with the help of Holy Spirit. The earlier you embrace the process, the quicker you can confidently walk in your calling.

I believe our preparation season doesn't happen all at once but occurs over and over again as we walk deeper and deeper in our calling.

We all know how this part of Esther's story ends. Esther found favour with the King, because she passed her intense preparation period. The King set the royal crown on her head and she was chosen to be the Queen.

God wants to set His royal crown on your head. But are you willing to pay the price to get your crown? Are you willing to go through the preparation stage, embrace the process and not give up along the way?

Reflections:

1. What season am I in? Do I seem to be going through a tough time that looks like I am being stripped of certain things or people?

2. What mindsets, habits, behaviours, and character traits, has God been revealing to me lately that I need to let go of?

3. What do I need to do to embrace this preparation stage I am in?

FIND YOUR STRIDE, WRITE YOUR STORY

Story 2

Here is the story of a lady who successfully navigated a season of preparation:

Hello, my name is Emilola. Writing this seems surreal - writing my confidence story! To be frank, I should probably call it my-ongoing-journey-to-confidence story.

I am married to a special guy and I'm a mum of two inspiring children. My first pregnancy ended in the death of a full-term baby. It was a harrowing time in our lives, as she was a much longed for baby. The months and years following that heartbreak drove me to lean more into God. I have always kept a diary/ journal since becoming a Christian at the age of 12. However, in that season God opened His Word to me like never before, and thus changed my journaling experience forever.

The journey

I have always been a creative person; writing poems and articles in my university days, taking part in poetry exhibitions at work. However, in that season my writings took a deeper direction. Most of what I wrote was for personal edification, occasionally voiced to close friends. I always dreamed of being a published novelist.

A couple of years after our sad loss, in 2010, one of the judges at work (*I work in the legal profession*) wanted to put up a summer art exhibition. I was interested, and encouraged by her, I submitted my writings. The general feedback was positive and that spurred me on to start writing poetry again.

Although I was keeping a journal, I had lost the desire to write poems because of all I had experienced personally, until that summer exhibition came along.

I began to desire more strongly to be published, though I didn't know how. In my own thoughts I kept having the idea that I was made for more.

Frustratingly, I didn't know what this 'more' was. I had been praying as well, on and off, for God to show me what I should be doing. In fact, that frustrated feeling was a large part of what I felt whilst on my third maternity leave. When I returned to work in summer of 2014, I still carried those thoughts within me.

One Saturday morning, I was about to start my devotion and I said to God, I don't know what to do, I want to write a book of poetry and I also want to write a devotional (a desire I had since I was 15). I should mention here that although my educational background was law, I didn't really want to continue on that path as I sought for a career/ job that would easily fit around my family, as my husband had a legal career too. So I ended up working in the civil service but I still felt unfulfilled.

As I part prayed and part moaned in my room that Saturday morning, I heard God's voice clear as day, deep in my heart – *"Then write a book that's part devotional, part poetry."* I immediately thought of reasons why I couldn't, no money set aside, little time and energy, while simultaneously saying out loud *"I can't write a part devotional, part poetry book!"*

Then He simply asked, *"why not?"* As I pondered on His reply, I asked myself why not, and then I said yes, I will. As soon as I said yes, peace descended, and I had clarity about what to do even if I didn't know how to go about it.

The awakening

Shortly after, I received a phone call, which led to being sponsored to attend the *Super Working Mum* (SWM) weekend retreat for Christian working mums in 2015. On the first night of the retreat, we watched a movie titled *Unconditional*; Samantha Crawford, an illustrator and writer who is happily married, loses her husband in a senseless and tragic killing one night. After a series of events, which start on that fateful night, she is reunited with a childhood friend. The friend now cares for and works with children from disadvantaged backgrounds.

Without giving too much away from the movie, Sam discovers this friend of hers is also suffering from severe kidney disease. He finds out that because of her pain, she no longer writes and has given up. As he draws his dying breath, he tells her this, *"Find your stride, Sam, write your story, it matters."*

As I watched this scene, it was as if everything froze, and those words hit me in my soul as if God was talking directly to me. I burst into tears, huge body racking sobs. *"Find your stride. Write your story, it matters."* Although I had received direction, I had been wrestling with thoughts of who cares what I write, there are so many people who are writers already, what do I have to write anyway?

"Write your story, it matters."

After the movie, I headed back to my hotel room, still feeling God's nearness. The following day, I had a 20-minute one to one session with Detola. She identified ideal times in my day to write. This was on the train, to and from work. She brushed aside my worries about lack of funds – *"God will provide the means"*, she said. She asked me to set a date for publishing the book. With huge unexpressed doubts, I picked a date 12 months later. The whole weekend retreat was one of divine appointment and confirmation.

God did provide! 10 months later, my first part devotional and part poetry book - *Springs of Living Water* was published. That great achievement gave me the courage to speak to people about my gift - *writing to encourage.*

The growth

One of the main challenges I had to overcome was not waiting until I looked the part or had everything I needed to step out. Being in the company of Kingdom minded women via *Super Working Mum Academy*, who were all on their different journeys helped a great deal.

In 2016, on a 3-month *Manifest Your Dreams* mastermind session facilitated by Detola, I started and completed the first draft of my second devotional - *Hope, my soul's anchor.* Eight months later, the book was published in spite of deep personal challenges at the time.

One thing I have found since recognising God's call to write and influence people through what He gives me is the deep sense of knowing that I am in His plan for my life. Subsequently, speaking opportunities to teach His Word and to share have opened up to me.

I am also learning to continually step outside my comfort zone in the ministry and the marketplace. I have exhibited my books and crafts at Christmas fairs and conferences for women. In 2017, I also undertook the *Digital Transformation Programme* created by Detola and successfully built my first website, www.thewellspringplace.com giving me a platform to reach more people with His Word.

Would I say that I am now confident? Not entirely, but part of being confident is to *'do it'* whatever your *'it'* is, even if you have to do it afraid and unsure. I still don't think I have everything I need to do what I need to do. However, when I look back, I realise God has done so many amazing things through me and to me. None of those things I thought I lacked prevented those amazing things from happening.

It's great to feel absolutely confident about what you do, or the way you do what you do, but until that happens don't dare let the lack of confidence stop you from finding your stride or writing your story. It definitely matters that you do.

CHAPTER 8

EMBRACE YOUR
UNIQUE PROJECT

O ver the next few chapters of this book, let us continue to delve deeper into Esther's story of God's calling on her life.

After Esther passed the test in her preparation period, she became queen. She had been promoted from the harem to the palace. Now she could breathe! Phew! However, she still didn't know what God had in store for her in form of a unique project. I imagine her doing her queenly duties on a daily basis and just getting on with life. She didn't know what was coming.

Remember Esther had kept her identity a secret as her uncle instructed her to; there is a lesson for us all here. Sometimes, you need to be discreet about what God is sharing with you. It is not everything God tells you, that you need to share, except God permits you to. A lot of projects, dreams, and visions have been prematurely aborted because they were shared with the wrong people. Being discreet and discerning is key when it comes to confidently manifesting God's calling on your life.

Esther was now in the place of affluence, enjoying her life and things were beginning to work out for her. Finally, it looked like she had gotten a break from life's issues. However, there was a bigger test waiting for Esther as the Queen. Haman, the King's right-hand man posed a big threat to her and her people; because of Haman, the King decided to get rid of all the Jews.

The truth is the more challenges you overcome on your journey;

the more problems will come your way. It never ends. However, the more prepared you are, the greater your ability to deal with problems as we find in the case of Esther.

The more challenges you overcome on your journey; the more problems will come your way.

Esther was faced with a dilemma. Should she go to the King without being called and risk dying and losing everything including her life? Or should she hide and let things slide hoping she will survive the coming attack?

Esther tried to dodge this one and come up with an excuse, but good old Uncle Mordecai warned her: "*Do not think that because you are in the king's house you alone of all the Jews will escape. For if you remain silent at this time, relief and deliverance for the Jews will arise from another place, but you and your father's family will perish. And who knows but that you have come to your royal position for such a time as this?*" Esther 4:13 – 14 (NIV)

Her day to step up confidently and to deliver on this big project had come. Thank God she passed the test. She rose up to the occasion and asked for reinforcement from God and the support of her people. She didn't try to do this on her own. The best part was even her maids were loyal and trustworthy enough that they joined her in fasting.

As part of your calling, you will have various projects to deliver. Who is in your corner? Who do you surround yourself with? I am referring to your friends, business partners, even your support system at home.

Your support system matters

As a mother, do not take for granted the people that take care of your children. For when you are out and about delivering that special assignment of God, you need people you can trust to watch over your family. I realised this on my journey.

I always took for granted the nannies I employed. Yes, I prayed about it but just to cover my bases. However, one day Abba began to tell me I needed to pay more attention. Whoever I bring into my home to help support me with my children needed to be in alignment with His plans and purpose for me. They cannot be of a different spirit as this may hinder my own calling, or they may be a source of distraction, or a negative influence on my children.

Coincidentally, a few of my friends had told me they had experienced the same awareness, and therefore had let go of nannies that were not in alignment with God's agenda for them. That gave me some relief knowing I wasn't the only one experiencing this kind of upheaval, as initially, I thought I was weird for letting my *'good'* nanny go when Abba asked me to.

God's ways are not our ways and if anything will stand in the way of His calling on our lives, He will bring it to our attention. It is now left to us to obey or not.

Another nugget from this part of Esther's story is when it is time to make a stand on what you believe, do you take a stand or make excuses? When people are threatening your God-given project, what do you do?

When people criticise your calling or your project, do you hide or do you take a stand for God? When the *'Hammans'* appear mightily against you and the God you represent, do you back down and surrender or do you see this as an opportunity to follow through?

I remember a lovely client who I helped with self-publishing her book. She heard from God on what to write and so she did. She then gave it to a few people to read for their endorsement. However, some of the feedback was that it had too many scriptures and was too *'Christian'* and would not appeal to a wider audience.

This bothered her and for a few days she wondered if she should make some changes to the book. However, when she mentioned it during one of our sessions, I encouraged her to stick to what the Lord told her to do and not be concerned about what anyone had to say.

She decided not to make any changes and now that she has published her book, she has received encouraging feedback from the people who needed to hear what she had to say. Isn't that amazing?

I also experienced similar criticism when I wrote my first book: *Super Working Mum, Living and Loving Life to the Fullest*. I must say I was a bit anxious about how women would receive the content of the book. But to God's glory a lot of women have come back with testimonies of how the book has helped them.

Because I had experienced and overcome similar criticism, I was able to help my mentee stay on track and not get discouraged by what the critics had to say.

When God gives you a project in line with your calling to deliver, your goal is to obey His instruction. He is your audience of One. Some people will have comments to make and some may even ridicule you, but don't let that stop you from taking a stand. We will discuss more on this in the next chapter.

Again, we know how the story ends with Esther. She found favour in the sight of God and with her husband, the King, and because of her confidence and bravery, she and her people were delivered.

There is someone out there waiting to be delivered from darkness because of you. Who is depending on you to make a stand so that they are delivered from oppression or depression?

Remember God's calling on your life is not about you; it is about the people God wants you to help.

Jesus says in Revelation 3:11 (NLT) *"I am coming soon. Hold on to what you have, so that no one will take your crown."*

Don't let anyone, any mindsets, or attitudes take away your crown. Your crown is what has set you apart for your calling. Your crown has elevated you to a higher level. Do not let your past, present situation, the world, pressures, lack of money etc. stop you from confidently manifesting God's calling on your life.

Reflections:

1. What projects has God given me to do? (Prayerfully decide who to share with)

2. What support system do I have in place to help me with the projects God has assigned to me?

3. Is it the right support system?

CHAPTER 9

DO AS INSTRUCTED

We are still on the topic of embracing your project. In the last chapter, we looked at how Esther confidently fulfilled the calling on her life to save her people. In this chapter, I would like us to dig deeper into how this applies to us.

One thing that can cause us to doubt is not being sure of what to do or being confused about the daily action steps you should be taking to fulfill your unique assignment and live out God's calling over your life. To combat this, I recommend following Jesus' example as described in the book of John.

This is one book of the Bible every believer should read over and over again. Unlike the books of Matthew, Mark and Luke that talk mainly about what Jesus did, John talks a lot about the person of Jesus in relation to the Father.

In almost all the chapters of the book of John, Jesus consistently made statements such as[4]:

"I do what I see my Father do"

"My teaching is not mine, but from The One who sent me"

"I do not speak on my own authority, but the Father who dwells in me does His works"

"I only do what the Father has instructed me to do"

You are a spirit; you have a soul that lives in your body. The correct order is for instruction to flow from your spirit to your soul and then to your body. They should always be in alignment. However, it is possible for your body and soul to desire something different from your spirit. As a born again child of God, your spirit is interested in what God's spirit wants and so you always have to bring your body and soul into alignment with your spirit man.

You are a spirit; you have a soul that lives in your body.

Yes, Jesus and God are one but with different personalities. Jesus, on earth, could have decided to do whatever He wanted to do, but He laid down His desires and did only what God, the Father instructed Him to do.

Despite the criticism from the Pharisees, the rejection from His brothers, people trying to stone Him, He was not moved because He knew He had His Father's backing and His priority was to do only what God asked Him to do.

Jesus knew that He was on assignment on this earth. He knew that His time in the earthly realm was limited; as a result, He stayed focused on His assignment.

In trying to live out God's calling, we need to follow Jesus' example daily. A friend of mine, refers to this as your *"Noah's ark project."*

When God instructed Noah to build the ark, God gave him specific instructions on how the ark should be built. Right down to what material to build the ark with, to the length, height and breadth of the ark, to the number of decks and down to the number of people and animals that were permitted to enter the ark.

I believe one of the reasons God gave Noah such specifics was because the ark had to withstand the big flood coming; if Noah had gone off to build an ark based on his own intellect or made the ark 250 feet long instead of 450 feet long[5], he and his family may have also been destroyed in the flood.

I remember when God gave me the vision for *Super Working Mum* (SWM), I felt at the time he wanted SWM to cater to

Christian mothers but in my intellect, I thought doing what God said won't be fair or right and non-Christians shouldn't be excluded. To be honest, I was afraid. I didn't want to be labeled as a fanatic, so I opened it up to everyone.

We had a Facebook group of over 4,000 people where I shared encouragement. It was an interactive group but deep down I knew something was missing. Firstly, when God gave me a message for the group, I always toned it down so that the non-Christians in the group wouldn't feel excluded and again I didn't want to be labeled as overly spiritual.

I was very concerned about my reputation and this was impacting my confidence in living out my assignment and obeying God fully. For a whole year, I felt like I had hit a ceiling. I wasn't moving any further and wasn't making as much impact as I should have been making. This was when Abba made it clear that I needed to go back to the specifications He gave me from the onset.

It was a very tough decision to make, but with tears in my eyes, I shut down the Facebook group and started a new group just for Christian mums. A part of me was still worried about being judged and labeled, but I felt so much peace and confidence to start afresh. Of course, this decision affected a number of relationships, not everyone migrated to the new group and I was criticised for my actions. However, I had to obey the Father, my audience of One, in order to move forward confidently.

I am grateful I made the move because things began to turn around, the women in my nation, who God wanted me to help, started coming to me in their numbers.

In fact, a few of them have said to me that they were in the previous group and even though it was a nice community, it didn't meet their specific needs. However, with the change of direction, the issues they were facing were dealt with head on, and they began to experience real transformation in their lives from the inside out. Glory to God!

These women needed help with birthing their God-given dreams whilst dealing with the challenges of life. These women needed help with growing spiritually so they could be in a better position to be the best wife and mum and also be a blessing to the nations God had called them to, through their own unique assignment.

This was the original assignment Abba gave me and even though I went off track for a few years, I am thankful that His mercy guided me back.

Sadly, some people till date, especially close to me, believe I made the wrong decision, but I know in my heart I didn't. I am at peace with the choice I made.

One day it actually became clearer to me, when I looked at the lives of the women I have helped by the grace of God. They have had different assignments to serve Christians and non-Christians alike. My calling is to help and empower Christian mothers (women) to birth their God-given dreams so that they can, in turn, help whomever it is God has called them to help, whether in the marketplace, in ministry, in their businesses etc.

I share my story to reinforce to you that God's calling on your life is very unique and different from mine. People might have meaningful and well thought out suggestions as to how you should build your *'Noah's ark'*, but the question is does it align with what God told you?

Whose instructions are you following? God's, yours, other people's, society's? You may be at a point where you are distracted and confused. You may seem to have hit a ceiling and not making as much progress or impact as you should be making. It is time to go back to God and ask Him to remind you of His specific instructions for you. Ask Him each day what His agenda is for you, then trust and obey.

I assure you that when you get in line with what the Father is saying, you will be empowered to slay doubt. Your confidence will return, and you will begin to see transformation in the lives of the people He has called you to serve.

Reflections:

Ask yourself:

1. What is my 'Noah's ark' project that God has given me to deliver and to whom?

2. Am I embracing this project fully and obeying God's instruction to the letter?

3. What do I need to change to align to God's instruction?

Action steps:

1. Write down your thoughts from the reflections above and take one action today to do what God is saying.

OWNING MY CALLING

Story 3

This is a story of a lady who took a while to recognise and own God's calling on her life.

I am Diane Oredope, wife to one wonderful man and mother to two amazing children who keep me grounded.

It is Ok to work for others

I am a pharmacist and have a PhD so I am often called Dr Diane. I am the lead pharmacist for the healthcare-associated infections (HCAI) and antimicrobial resistance (AMR) division, National Infection Service, Public Health England, and the deputy chair of the English Surveillance Programme for Antimicrobial Utilisation and Resistance (ESPAUR). I am passionate about pharmacy and believe that my calling is within the workplace.

Through the grace of God, I have had the opportunity to project lead the development of a number of national Antimicrobial Stewardship initiatives. I also led the development and implementation evaluation of the Antibiotic Guardian campaign and continually provide significant contributions to AMR related behaviour insights, interventions and analysis in Public Health England. I now support colleagues across the Globe, especially the African continent, to tackle antibiotic resistance.

Currently, I do not have a defined ministry or business. However, over the years, I have dabbled in business and learnt great skills that I bring to and use in my workplace. It has taken me a while to get comfortable and to own God's calling in my career.

In paying attention to staying in my lane, I now know that it is OK to work for others. I have had to overcome self-doubt and

70

worry which came from feeling like the odd one out. In the circles/communities I was in, everyone seemed to have a ministry, business or side gig. Also, many things I read on social media seemed to infer that *"having multiple sources of income is critical in the new era and it is empowering"*. However, now, I have learnt and become comfortable knowing that we have all been called differently.

It has also been challenging being a mum of two young children (now 10 and 7) and working full time (often more hours than full time). I have learnt some useful time management strategies from SWM Academy that have helped me maximise my time at work and at home. Also, SWM Academy has been my lifeline or SOS call group several times when things have gotten overwhelming and I needed fellow ladies to stand with me in prayers.

Stay in your own lane

My advice for people struggling to own their calling is *work to stay in your own lane*. Realise that there are seasons for everything. In a few years' time, I might be released or believe it is time to have a side gig once again or even start my own business. But in this season, I am where I should be.

Find a community of others - be willing to share your experience. In sharing, you learn so much and you would find people who can support you. Most importantly, *pray and trust God* whilst putting one foot in front of the other.

The people that I believe have been impacted by me staying in my lane and determining to be the best that God has called me to be (*and this excludes my family - husband, children, parents and siblings because for me they are number 1*) include pharmacists. Particularly young pharmacists who I mentor and those who I don't know personally but who follow my posts and are inspired.

Also, families and members of the public have been impacted

through the national campaign - which helps increase understanding about the challenges of antibiotics resistance - that God helped me create and which I still lead 5 years on.

Bring God to the workplace

I am constantly in awe of the places that God brings me to, and the platforms He has given me and continues to lead me to. For instance, meeting and discussing with health ministers of countries, delivering two TEDx talks that I did not apply for, but was nominated for by people who are not even within my circle.

Whilst most of them are not the place to preach (*I don't preach in any case*), they do mean that more people are open and willing to listen when I do speak. It also means that when, for example, I put out a tweet giving God the glory - more people see this on social media.

My platform is not your typical pulpit or ministry, but I am very aware of the responsibility I have and carry due to my role and position, and I bring God into this. One simple example is that before I go to any meeting or event – I specifically pray for those attending that they will experience God's love/smile through my presence and if anyone is sad, that somehow, I will have a word of encouragement for them.

CHAPTER 10

ARE YOU BEING SELFISH?

Y ou may be wondering, what does selfishness have to do with slaying doubt and manifesting your calling? Well…a lot! And this is what this chapter is all about.

Firstly, let's define the word selfish. According to the dictionary, it means, *"lacking consideration for other people; concerned chiefly with one's own personal profit or pleasure."*

Another word that describes selfish is self-centered, which means *"preoccupied with oneself and one's affairs, concerned solely with one's own desires, needs, or interests."*

What are some signs that you are acting selfishly?

1. When you are always concerned about yourself and your comfort.

2. When all you think or pray about is what concerns you and your immediate family.

3. When you place more importance on what people think of you rather than on doing God's work.

4. When God gives you a message for someone, but you are scared of telling him or her because you might look like silly.

5. When you don't use the gifts and talents God has given you because of fear of criticism or stepping on people's toes.

I can go on and on, but this gives you an idea of when you are acting with selfish motives. Many of us are so concerned about our reputation, or about what others think, or about being ridiculed or rejected, or about making a mistake in public that we would rather hide and live miserably than step into our calling.

I remember when I started *Super Working Mum*; I used a pseudonym *'Aloted'* to identify myself - that's my name written backwards in case you couldn't tell. I was happy to write and put my picture out there, but I didn't want my real name out in the public domain. My excuse was that I didn't want to mix my career with my ministry/business life, but the actual truth was I wanted to hide behind a fake name.

I wrote my first and second book with my pseudonym, however a few years later, I heard Abba say it was time to get rid of the pseudonym and start using my real name. Boy! That was a big struggle for me... I felt exposed! I felt like people were now going to know the real me. I went back and forth with God over this, but His instruction did not change. It was time to come out, so I did, and nobody died of shock as a result!

I know this example might sound trivial and this is not to say that using a pseudonym is wrong, but sometimes God can decide to strip you of anything that is a false refuge in your life, for the work He wants to do and for the people He wants you to help.

He can tell you to share that horrid story from your past because it will set someone else free. He can tell you to call someone you haven't spoken to in years, which might deliver him or her from committing suicide. Whatever the case may be you have to get over yourself and get in line with what Abba is saying.

Another sign of selfishness is when all you can think about is money. I have had people say to me, *"I will do what God wants me to do after I have made enough money."* So they stay in a job or business not in alignment with God's plan for them because of the *'extra money'* they want to make. Sadly, you can never make 'enough' money. You will always want more, and if you make your life all about making money, this will distract you from God's calling. This can lead to frustration, as the Bible says you cannot serve God and money, you need to choose one.

If you choose to serve God, He will always make provision for your calling.

So, whom will you choose to serve? Will it be God or money? If you choose to serve God, He will always make provision for your calling. He can never leave you stranded or in lack. When you make God's business your business, He provides much more than you need. He is the one who has given you the ability to create wealth, so money will always find its way to you as you make an impact.

However, if you choose to serve money, it will fail you because it is unreliable. Money has wings and can fly away[6]. You will find that you are always striving and toiling to make money and you can't even really enjoy it when you get it.

Quality not Quantity

In John 10:11 – 13 (AMP) Jesus drives home this point:

"I am the Good Shepherd. The Good Shepherd lays down His [own] life for the sheep. But the hired man [who merely serves for wages], who is neither the shepherd nor the owner of the sheep, when he sees the wolf coming, deserts the flock and runs away; and the wolf snatches the sheep and scatters them. The man runs because he is a hired hand [who serves only for wages] and is not concerned about the [safety of the] sheep."

We should desire to be like Jesus who laid down His life for His sheep, in our case, the nation He has assigned to us. Our priority should be to care for our nation. If we serve only because of money, we are likely to abandon God's calling when trouble comes.

When God told me to start weekend retreats for women, the first two were successful and popular. By the third retreat, the number of people interested was nothing to write home about. Only a handful of people signed up and I was upset. I felt like canceling the retreat due to the few sign-ups. When I finally remembered to go to Holy Spirit about it, He told me I had made the retreats about me. It was no longer about the people coming. I was acting selfishly thinking about myself and how it would look if people didn't turn up. I was also thinking about the money I could potentially lose after all the planning and effort I had put into organising the retreat. I learned a big lesson that day. Abba made me realise that it wasn't about the quantity of people that attended, but the quality of the retreat. It wasn't about the number of people or the money, but about the impact. Since then, I don't get agitated about the number of people that attend the *Super Working Mum* retreats.

Yes, I do my part by sharing about the retreat and planning for a great time, but I leave the rest in God's hands. My belief now is that the right people who need to attend a particular retreat will be led to come and will leave refreshed and blessed. Ever since I took myself out of the equation, my team and I plan the retreats effortlessly.

As at the time of writing this book, we have had 13 retreats in total and God has always manifested Himself powerfully at each retreat. Women in attendance experience transformation in their lives and I have never been out of pocket running the retreats. Win-win all round for everyone.

These words from a devotion I read may help us put things in perspective.

"God never gives us a calling without providing all we need to get it done, and that includes time and emotional capacity.

If we aren't able to get it done, despite our best efforts, then He has a different plan in mind--perhaps a different person or a different time. Let's listen when the Holy Spirit gently calls us to set certain things aside and trust that He has them in His control."

- Author Unknown

Are you trying to force God's hand or trying to manipulate a situation to go a certain way? Are you worried about the money needed to do God's work and is this stressing you out? I encourage you to hand it over to God (your CEO), let Him lead the way and obey any instructions He gives you.

Anytime you find yourself thinking about yourself or getting worried about what people will think or say when it comes to walking in your calling, sharing your story, using your gifts or living in purpose, ask yourself:

Who is benefiting from me not stepping out*? No one*

Who will this affect? *The people who are in need of hope, healing or restoration, or those who need to know God's solution for their problem.* Anytime God asks you to speak up, remove yourself from the equation and speak. There have been occasions God will drop a message for someone in my spirit and I will feel weird about telling him or her, but when I do, I find it is just what he or she needed to hear. The more I step out in obedience, the more I slay doubt and my confidence rises. Sometimes you might get it wrong but that's fine. As long as you are operating from a place of love, learn from that experience but don't let that stop you in your tracks.

What has God asked you to do: *change your job, pray for someone at work, write a book or a song, start a business, start a blog, raise money for charity, start a ministry?*

Don't let selfishness or self-centeredness stop you…

Don't let what you think about yourself stop you…
Don't let what others think about you stop you….
Don't over-analyse things…
Stop thinking about your qualifications or lack of it, just do it!

Henry T. Blackaby once said, *"God does not call the qualified, He qualifies the called."* Think of Moses, Gideon, Samuel, and Jonah, in the Bible. They didn't have the required qualifications based on human standards, but God still chose to use them.

The only person that matters is the ONE who has sent you. At the end of the day, the glory (*and the criticism*) goes back to God.

Reflection:

1. What has God asked me to do but I have been afraid to step out on, due to fear of no resources or for other reasons?

Action step:

1. Today, I want you to lay down all those reasons at the feet of Jesus and ask Him for strength and wisdom for the next step to take now.

CHAPTER 11

FOCUS AND ENDURANCE

H ebrews 12:1-2 (NASB) says:
"Therefore, since we have so great a cloud of witnesses surrounding us, let us also lay aside every encumbrance and the sin which so easily entangles us, and let us run with endurance the race that is set before us, fixing our eyes on Jesus, the author and perfecter of faith, who for the joy set before Him endured the cross, despising the shame, and has sat down at the right hand of the throne of God."

As you embrace your project and run with the vision God has given you, focus and endurance are paramount.

Focus

As we have already established, God's calling on your life is bigger than you. It is such that will require different actions, steps or ideas for you to implement. Sometimes it could get confusing knowing which idea will bring you closer to fulfilling your calling and manifesting your God-given dreams. Some ideas will simply be distractions. You must be discerning to know if an idea is a distraction or the real deal.

There are good ideas and there are God ideas.

Firstly, realise that not every idea that is good is from God. There are *good ideas* and there are *God ideas*. To discover which ones are from God and not what has come from your flesh, or what everyone else is doing or saying or the most popular option out there, take all the options back to God, the key stakeholder in your project, and ask Him what idea you need to focus on right now.

This is what I like to call - *saying a bold prayer*. I must warn you not to say this prayer if you are not ready to hear what God has to say, because it is possible that God's answer may not align with what your flesh wants you to do. God's answer may not be the easiest option on the list. But thankfully His grace is sufficient for you.

Let me share one of my experiences with you.

I remember when I had to decide between working on two ideas that had come to my mind. One was to start work on creating the first journal in the *Super Working Mum* journal series, the other was to build my email list by creating and sharing a free resource online that would help women, and also make more women aware of the work I did.

Creating the journal was new and scary; therefore, I was reluctant to do anything about it. Building my email list was in my comfort zone and even though the process could be cumbersome I had done it several times. So my first choice was to build my email list, nevertheless, I took it to Abba and asked Him to make it clear to me which idea He wanted me to work on then. I sensed Him saying I needed to work on the journal, but I ignored the prompt.

That afternoon I decided to go with my choice, build my email list. It was meant to be a free video series on self-care for mothers. I recorded about three videos that day on my phone and was really proud of myself. In the process of trying to transfer the videos to my laptop and upload onto YouTube, I lost all three videos.

In fact, my phone crashed! I was able to recover all the other videos and pictures on my phone except those three videos. I was really upset and asked God why that happened. His answer- *"You asked Me what idea to work on."*

That was a wake-up call for me. Let's just say I got right to work on the journal. Several grueling but exciting months later, the *Living Amazed Journal* became a reality, glory to God.

Now I am not saying God crashed my phone (or maybe He did who knows!) but I am saying because I took both ideas to Him and asked Him to make it clear to me, He made it really clear to me especially since I had gone off to do my own thing. When things like this happen, I see them as *"God saved me from myself"* moments.

Remember God called you. He gave you the vision, so He knows what ideas you need to be working on per time to move closer to fulfilling that vision.

The truth is other ideas will cross your mind when you are working on a particular God idea. The journal project took months to complete, and was not without its challenges, but I stayed true to it. Anytime I reached a blockade in the process, I went back to God and He showed me what to do. Yes, I worked on other activities but I didn't invest time on any other major big projects at the same time. Multi-tasking is not the answer, staying focused is.

The devil, your enemy, won't be happy when he sees you are determined to do what God has asked you to do, so he might bring *'bright shining objects'* your way in the form of other fantastic ideas, to get you off course. You will be presented with ideas that seem like they could help you get to where you are going but they are merely distractions. Not all good ideas are God ideas.

Determine with the help of God to stay focused and see that idea through to completion. If led by Holy Spirit check with your mentor, coach or a trusted friend. Be determined to run the race that has been set before you. Don't just be a starter, be a finisher.

I remember one of my mentees who was working on launching a new program in her coaching practice. Everything was set to go, then she said to me one day that there was this new brilliant business that people were doing that would help generate income and she was thinking of doing that business so she could inject the money she makes from that business into her coaching practice.

Even though it sounded like a great strategic move, I helped her realise that this new program she was about to launch was going to generate income. We both came to the conclusion that the time she would invest in this alternative business was time away from working on the launch of her program. I suggested that she should channel the excitement and energy she was feeling for the alternative idea into getting new clients to sign up for her new program rather than getting distracted with this new business idea that had nothing to do with her calling. She took my advice and was able to successfully launch the program which helped the women who needed her help.

Everything you do on a daily basis must be in line with your calling. Anything done outside of this is a waste of time and simply a distraction.

All that said, other God ideas might come to you as you work on a big project. So that you do not get overwhelmed and weighed down, have an *'ideas notebook'* for these God ideas. When they come to you, write them down. That way you have captured them and can always come back to them when the time is right.

To be a finisher and not just a starter, you need to stay accountable to someone. This could be your coach/mentor or an accountability group with people who are also focusing on achieving the goal/dream God has laid on their heart. This will help with boosting your confidence and with keeping you focused. When you are going off course, the person/people you are accountable to can help guide you back.

Lastly, remain sensitive to what the Holy Spirit is saying per time. When He says, *"go this way"* you go, when He says *"pause"* you pause. Let Him be your guide.

It was a good thing Abraham was paying attention to the angel when He told him not to sacrifice Isaac, if not, he would have been following old instructions instead of following instructions for the present.

Endurance

According to the Cambridge English dictionary, endurance means *"the ability to keep doing something difficult, unpleasant, or painful for a long time."*

The word *Endurance* used in Hebrews 12:2 is the Greek word *'hypomonē'* which describes someone *"who is not swerved from his deliberate purpose and his loyalty to faith and piety by even the greatest trials and sufferings."*

From this definition of endurance, it is clear that living a life of purpose, and obeying the call of God on your life is not an easy task. If it were easy, a lot of people on earth would be on the path of purpose and living the life they were called to live.

Like I mentioned a few times, God's calling on your life is bigger than you. It requires you to calmly and bravely abide in your lane, so that you can do what you were born to do while fighting off doubts, insecurities, ill treatment and day-to-day challenges.

If we follow the example of Jesus, his assignment on earth was to lay down His life for all mankind. That was a very difficult assignment to undertake but the Bible tells us in Hebrews 12:2 (NASB) that " ...*for the joy set before Him, [Jesus] endured the cross, despising the shame, and has sat down at the right hand of the throne of God.*"

Jesus focused on the reward when He died on the cross. He didn't focus on the cross.

What was the joy set before Jesus? According to Hebrews 12 verses 2 and 10, the joy was to be seated in the place of honor at the right-hand side of God's throne and seeing the sons of men reconciled to God. Jesus focused on the reward when He died on the cross. He didn't focus on the cross.

He didn't dwell on the obstacles or shame that came His way. He didn't quit when this gruesome task became really hostile, lonely and painful. He looked past the horror of the cross and saw what was beyond the cross. He knew where He was going and that kept Him going.

On your life's journey, just like Jesus, you will experience setbacks, embarrassment, shame, pain, and suffering. Instead of focusing on the challenges, look beyond them in your mind and think about the joy that is set before you. This joy could include:

1. The lives of people who will be transformed through you.

2. The ripple positive effect on their families and generations to come.

3. Souls that will be won for God's Kingdom.

4. Healing, freedom and liberation of souls.

When the enemy attacks your mind, health, finances, marriage, children, etc., this is not the time to give up and throw a pity party. It is the time to confront the attack with a declaration of God's words. It is a time to declare victory through praise and a time to encourage others.

You are a soldier in God's army

Because God has called you, it means you are a soldier in His army. Therefore, you *CANNOT* be entangled in worldly affairs.

Think back to any soldier you have seen whether in real life or in the movies. We observe how they carry themselves: There is an air of authority and pride around them. They don't mess around or discuss irrelevant matters with mere civilians. They carry out orders given to them by their commanding officer, no matter what. They are committed to their course.

This is how we should live out God's calling on our lives. We cannot afford to be petty about certain issues anymore, we cannot be shallow thinkers, we cannot get offended, and we cannot worry. No, we CANNOT.

Our **focus** must be on **pleasing** our commanding officer at all times.

- A soldier is not fearful or in hiding: *It is time to stop hiding...time to break away from that fearful mindset.*

- A soldier knows who his commanding officer is: *Do you know who your commanding officer is? Do you know to whom you belong?*

- A soldier is not involved in frivolous discussions: *What frivolous discussions do you need to stop having today?*

- A soldier doesn't care what you think about him because he has work to do: *Are you busy living in purpose or still wondering what people are saying about you?*

- A solider does not get overly sensitive, or upset over every tiny issue: *Are you easily offended by what people do or do not do?*

This is a wake-up call for us all. Let us get rid of fear, bitterness, anger, pride, and pettiness. Let us seek to please our heavenly Father.

It is time to get FOCUSED and FEARLESS! It is time to slay DOUBT.

I will not pretend for a second that living like a solider for Christ is easy. It is a daily commitment we need to make, of laying down our flesh and partnering with Holy Spirit. It is about allowing Holy Spirit to unravel and remove all the different layers of negative mindsets in us.

We cannot do any of these in our own strength, but through the supernatural strength of Holy Spirit, if we ask for His help, WE CAN, one day at a time.

Reflection:

1. How can I change my focus from my challenges to the reward coming?

2. What joy has been set before me that I can focus on?

3. In what ways can I start behaving like solider in God's army?

KNOW AND FOCUS ON YOUR NATION

Story 4

This is a story of a lady who is embracing her unique project and focusing on the implementation of her God-given assignment.

My name is Ifueko Omoniyi, a Certified Health Coach & Nutrition consultant and the founder of *Lifestyle by KoKo*.

My calling is to inspire women to develop healthy eating habits and teach them how to achieve a well-balanced, healthy lifestyle. It is my goal to ensure that eating clean is made easy, appealing, exciting and most importantly stress-free.

A journey of self-discovery

My journey as a nutrition and lifestyle expert started with my passion for healthy living. Growing up, I struggled with eating because of the fear of weight gain. I was very conscious of my weight and did not realise that my unhealthy eating habits had developed into an eating disorder.

My unhealthy ways of eating so as to continue being slim were ineffective after I gave birth to my second child. It felt like the fat I had been avoiding, came to wage war on my body. I gained a lot of weight to the extent that I lost confidence in myself and decided to stay indoors for over one year.

After a year of hiding, I embarked on a personal journey of self-discovery to gain back my confidence.

I was able to get back in shape and gained back my confidence after discovering that food can either make or break us. I learnt how to eat right and out of curiosity and excitement, started teaching and helping women understand their bodies and food, to help them gain back their confidence.

Seeking help

I was not sure if this passion was my calling until after I got a confirmation from the Holy Spirit at the *Super Working Mum* retreat in 2016. I kept looking for excuses not to adhere to this calling by telling myself I was not fit for this purpose of helping women.

The more questions I asked, the more clarification I got from the Holy Spirit. Even with the confirmation from the Holy Spirit, I still wasn't bold enough to step out of my comfort zone to embrace my calling. I was really concerned about what people would say, forgetting that this was a calling from God. Also because I had other businesses I was managing, heeding to the call of helping women attain their health and weight goals was challenging for me.

I knew there were obstacles ahead, so I had to seek help to strategise on how to manage all these businesses. I joined the *Super Working Mum Academy*. Later on, I enrolled for the *Manifest Your Dream* mastermind program (MYD) for three months to help me stay accountable, followed by the *Digital Transformation Program* (DTP) to help me with growing my business online. By enrolling on these programs with Detola, I grew, and I was able to make strategic plans on how to merge all my businesses together.

One of the major challenges I faced after stepping out was the rejection I got from people. I learnt from DTP how to create a niche and focus on it. I also realised that my product was not meant for everyone, but the people God has ordained for me to work with. This is what Detola calls *"Knowing your Nation"*.

The SWM Academy and the various other programs I enrolled on (as mentioned above) have played a great role in my journey of becoming who I am today and I am so grateful to God for this.

Stepping out of my comfort zone is one of my greatest achievements. Smiles have been put on faces because I said yes to my calling. The thought of some life-changing victories and testimonials from clients, gives me the extra strength to go on with this calling. Sometimes I wonder what would have become of these people with amazing victories and testimonials, if I had not taken that bold step to face my fears.

Believe in yourself

My advice to those that are lacking the confidence to step out is that they should believe in themselves and trust God to do His will in their lives. Sometimes in life, we shy away from God's calling over our lives because of some challenges and lack of confidence. We refuse to take the bull by the horn because of *'fear of the unknown'* or *'fear of what people will say'*. We forget that God has not given us the spirit of fear but a sound mind. He has made us to be solution providers through the power of the Holy Spirit at work in us.

Never doubt your ability or think that you are not ready for what God has called you to do.

Another piece of advice is to trust and leave it to God. Then see Him do wonders and fulfill His purpose in your life. Sometimes, the work of your hands might be irrelevant to some people, but it is simply because you were not called to them. So, do not feel discouraged or doubt the abilities that God has bestowed upon you.

You do not need everyone to believe in your vision or in what you do. The people that need you and your services are patiently waiting and will definitely locate you someday.

CHAPTER 12

INTIMACY WITH GOD

In the previous chapters, I have highlighted different strategies on how to recognise God's calling on your life, how to slay doubt, and how to confidently manifest what God has called you to do. I would like to emphasise that doing all of these requires that we see life from God's perspective. We are not just required to live out our calling but to develop intimacy with Abba Father.

They go hand in hand: responsibility and relationship.

It is important that we separate our own personal devotional time with God from our calling. We need a solid relationship with God to effectively carry out our responsibility on earth. We don't just want to be signposts for others or be disqualified after preaching to others as Paul mentioned in 1 Corinthians 9:27 (NKJV): "*But I discipline my body and bring it into subjection, lest, when I have preached to others, I myself should become disqualified.*"

Your Personal Time with God

I know many people pray on the go, but I think it is important that we take intentional time out to seek God's face.

It's like going on a date night with your spouse, spending quality time with your children or hanging out with your friends. God deserves our attention.

When Jesus was on earth, He spent quality time with God. It was from that place of intimacy He was able to pour into His disciples and the world. He also performed a lot of miracles after spending time with God.

Abba reveals more about our calling when we seek His face. He reveals His heart to us in the place of intimacy.

As wives, mothers, sisters, business owners, women in career, we give to and serve others daily: our husbands, children, friends, ministry, colleagues, clients, etc. When we do, our spiritual, emotional and physical resources get depleted. So we need to go back into His presence every day to get filled up again before we can give to others. Just like a phone battery needs charging every day, we need to get recharged to function at our best.

Our tank of joy needs filling up every day.

We live in evil and perilous times, with a lot of bad things happening all around us. Therefore, our tank of joy needs filling up every day. The joy of the Lord is our strength and in His presence is fullness of joy, so spending time with God will increase our joy.

God desires *'alone time'* with us. We should desire to grow in a personal relationship with Him above anything else. God had *alone time* with Moses, Joshua, David, Elijah, other prophets and even Jesus. Building intimacy with God rids our minds of distraction so that we can focus on Him and hear His Word throughout the day.

An outline

To give you an idea of what personal time with God may look like, I have given you an example of mine below. This is only an example and it changes from time to time depending on the season or Holy Spirit's leading.

When carving out your personal time, follow the leading of the Holy Spirit to guide you on what your time with Abba should be.

■ Background Worship Music such as Christian instrumentals,

or prophetic instrumental soaking music. This could be from YouTube or Amazon Music.

- I read a daily devotion and write down in my journal what God is saying. I use the *Living Amazed Journal*[5] during my time with Abba.

- Sometimes I read a book of the Bible if I am doing a particular study.

- I write in my journal an affirmation or confession from the Bible.

- I pray using scripture for different areas of my life. I do a daily declaration of specific promises of God for my family and I.

- I pray in tongues (I also do this on the go)

- I read a few chapters of any personal or spiritual growth book I am reading if I have time.

- I pray for others. There is a guide in the *Living Amazed Journal* that reminds me of which group of people I am praying for that day of the week.

Sometimes I just sit quietly, listen to music, or worship. Sometimes I engage my imagination and have a conversation with Jesus. I am moving away from sticking to a routine when it comes to my personal time with Abba Father, as I can be very routine-oriented. This is why I advise that even though it is good to have an outline flow with Holy Spirit every day.

Reflection:

1. What do I want my personal time with God to look like?

Action steps:

1. Write a plan with the help of Holy Spirit.

2. Use your plan as a guide but let Holy Spirit lead how your devotional time should go.

CHAPTER 13

HEBREW MINDSET
VS GREEK MINDSET

I first came across this concept in Shawn Bolz's book: *Keys to Heaven Economy: An Angelic Visitation from the Minister of Finance*[6], where he differentiates between the Hebrew and Greek mindset.

The Hebrew mindset is about having a holistic lifestyle where there is no compartmentalising or separating one area of life from the other e.g. work life, church life, family life, etc. It is such that all areas of life function as one and flows into one another.

On the other hand, in the Greek mindset, different personalities come into play in the different aspects of our lives. For example, we act one way at work; we act a different way at home, and another way at church or when we are with other believers. It is having, for example, a strategic mindset for our business or job but not applying that same mindset to other aspects of our lives.

The calling of God on our lives must apply to every aspect of our lives.

The Greek mindset is about hearing, thinking, analysing and studying. On the other hand, the Hebrew mindset is about seeing, feeling and experiencing God in His fullness on a daily basis, and experiencing God's presence in every aspect of our lives.

The calling of God on our lives must apply to every aspect of our lives. We don't just put on the *'calling hat'* for spiritual matters and not in our day-to-day living. As we navigate and grow through each season, our calling should flow to every area of our lives: our homes, finances, and relationships. Remember you are on earth for an assignment, so everything you do should flow from there.

God's desire is that we are whole in every aspect of our lives here on earth. This happens when we are authentic and align our spirit, soul, and body to God's purposes, when we apply the mind of Christ to every aspect of our lives.

If that job is not in alignment with your assignment, find a new job

If that business opportunity or speaking gig is not in alignment with your assignment, say no

If that relationship will derail you from your assignment, stay far away from it

If there is any area of our lives that is not in alignment with the purpose of God, we need to humbly bring that area to God to work on.

We need to constantly renew our minds, that is, think God thoughts. We need to constantly plead the blood of Jesus over our minds.

This is an ongoing sanctification process for every believer who wants to have an intimate relationship with God and confidently manifest God's calling on their lives.

Reflection:

1. What mindset do I currently have: Greek or Hebrew?

2. What area of my life is not in alignment with God's purpose?

Action steps:

1. Humbly bring any areas of your life that is not in alignment to God to work on.

YOUR NEXT STEPS

A s we come to a conclusion, I would like to encourage you to not just read this book, say wow, get excited and then go back to your old ways of thinking and living an average life. You have recognised the calling of God on your life and now I would love for you to take some next steps to confidently walk in your calling.

It is likely that you still have questions, you need more guidance with identifying what action steps you should be taking, or you need support to manifest God's calling on your life. You may also still need clarity on recognising what your calling is.

If this is you, there are so many ways I would love to walk alongside you on your journey. However, to kick-start the process, I would like to invite you to join the *Super Working Mum Academy* (SWMA) online community. This community has been designed for Christian mothers/women to get the support and motivation they need to MAXIMISE their time so that they can MANIFEST their God given dreams.

In SWM Academy, we have women from all over the world who are slaying doubt, and confidently manifesting God's calling on their lives. Throughout the book, I have shared stories and examples of some of the women in our community.

These are women just like you, confidently navigating the different seasons of life and staying on top. I know you will enjoy being a part of this community as these women will ginger you up, motivate you, hold you accountable and pray with you.

Apart from our thriving community, the SWM Academy has life changing online programs to show you how to maximise your time, how to manifest your dreams and also how to map out what your life purpose is. Go to www.academy.superworkingmum.com for all the details. After you have joined the Academy for a few months, we can then look at other specific ways to walk alongside you on your journey.

If you need further information before making a commitment to join us, then I invite you to explore the *Super Working Mum* website[7] and our YouTube channel[8]. Read some of the blog posts and watch some of the videos. Get the free report on *Maximising Your Time* on the website.

My desire is to see you live the life God intended for you on earth. Whatever you do, I implore you to make a decision today that will move you forward. You were designed to succeed. What you need now is the right skills and support to soar.

Come join me and other Super Working Mums on this journey of slaying doubt and manifesting God's calling!

RESOURCES MENTIONED IN THE BOOK

[1] Digital Transformation Program: http://academy.superworkingmum.com/digital-transformation-program

[2] Seven mountains of influence: http://7culturalmountains.org/

[3] Super Working Mum Academy: www.academy.superworkingmum.com

[4] Grace and Forgiveness by John and Carol Arnott: https://amzn.to/2WZDp94

[5] Living Amazed Journal: http://www.superworkingmum.com/living-amazed-journal.html

[6] Keys to Heaven's Economy: An Angelic Visitation from the Minister of Finance: https://amzn.to/2W2skmy

[7] Super Working Mum website: www.superworkingmum.com

[8] Super Working Mum YouTube Channel: www.youtube.com/c/Superworkingmum

Scriptures:

[1] John 14:12
[2] Esther 1:3
[3] Esther 2:16
[4] John 5:19, John 7:16, John 14:10, John 8:28
[5] Genesis 6:15
[6] Proverbs 23:5

Bible versions:

Please note that bible references in this book have been taken from the following versions:

New Living Translation
New American Standard Bible
The Amplified Bible
New King James Version
New International Version (Please note that this list may not be exhaustive.)

NOTE FROM THE AUTHOR

Thank you for buying this book. I would love this book to be read by as many Christian mums as possible, because I believe it will transform their minds and set them free from doubt and fear so they can confidently manifest God's calling on their lives.

If you enjoyed reading it, you can please help spread the word by doing the following:

Recommend It. Suggest this book to other mums in your circle of influence or buy it as a gift for others.

Talk About It. Mention it on Facebook, Twitter, or Instagram. Create a conversation about it using the hashtags #slaydoubt #manifestdreams #superworkingmum. You may also use the cover image as your profile picture on social networking sites.

Write About It. You can write about your thoughts from this book in an article or review it on your blog or someone's blog.

Discuss It. If you are part of a book club, recommend this book to be read in your book club and discuss the chapters.

Review It. Leave a review online. By leaving a review online, Amazon is likely to suggest this book to others to buy.

Many thanks for spreading the word.

ABOUT SUPER WORKING MUM

Super Working Mum is a global organisation that aims to help Christian Mothers who are overwhelmed maximise their time so that they can manifest their God given dreams.

SWM help women to achieve the above through one or more of the following ways:

Super Working Mum Facebook group

Super Working Mum Academy

Super Working Mum Weekend Retreats

Digital Transformation Program for Super Working Mums

Manifest Your Dreams 90 days mastermind sessions

Manifest Your Dreams VIP sessions

Empowering Mothers Annual Conference in September

For more information please visit www.superworkingmum.com

"You will find a 'tool' to tackle every 'nutty' issue of life you might face as a woman, wife and mother."

Get your copy on Amazon now!

To inquire about having Detola speak at your event, please visit the website and click on "speaking" under "Work with Detola"

Printed in Great Britain
by Amazon

40625112R00076